D1237519

TO

FROM

DATE

40 DAYS TO *Unwavering Hope*

DaySpring
LIVE YOUR FAITH

First Edition, November 2022

Published by:

21154 Highway 16 East
Siloam Springs, AR 72761
dayspring.com

Written by: Paige DeRuyscher
Cover Design by: Hannah Bedell

Printed in China
Prime: J9332
ISBN: 978-1-64870-843-5

Contents

Dear Friends,

I'm delighted that this book has found its way to you! My prayer in writing it was that many hearts would find lasting hope and reassurance in its pages.

How do we know our God is a God of hope? We see it everywhere in His Word and in our world, as He blazes trails that no one believed were possible; brings light into lives that were once lived in darkness and despair; shows up in places we'd never think to look, just to remind us that yes, we can trust Him, even when we have no idea how it's all going to play out.

How wonderful that we were created with the capacity to believe what we can't yet see—to look beyond challenging circumstances and envision brighter days. Our Maker knew what it would take for us to move through an unpredictable world with a deep sense of peace inside. He knew that our lives wouldn't be easy, but He made a way for them to be filled with goodness and love from beginning to end.

As you read these entries, answer the questions, and consider the suggestions that follow, I pray you will find encouragement that's specific to what you're facing in your life today, but also, a lasting sense of hope you can carry through all your days.

We each experience our lives with Jesus so personally and uniquely, but we all share that One, infinite Source of love—the love of our Heavenly Father. So, as we walk this path, we can truly say "we're all in this together," and I am grateful to be alongside you on the journey.

I am making a way
in the wilderness
and streams
in the wasteland.

ISAIAH 43:19 NIV

Christ Jesus, Our Hope

Have you ever really listened to how people talk about hope? Often it's referred to as a kind of ingredient they can add when they need a little extra *oomf* in life. Maybe when they're going through a hard time or when they'd really like to see a certain outcome, they might say things like: "*This is tough, but at least I have some* hope!" or "*I'm trying something new, so I'm just gonna* hope *for the best!*" What they may not realize in those moments is that they're actually talking about wishful thinking. But the hope God offers us is something altogether different; it has substance; it sustains us and transforms us, even as we wait to see how it will bear fruit fully in our lives. As Romans 5:5 (NLT) reminds us: "This hope will not lead to disappointment. For we know how dearly God loves us, because He has given us the Holy Spirit to fill our hearts with His love." The hope we have in Christ is not a now-and-then feeling—it's eternal. *It's the lens through which we can choose to see everything, every day*. We can stake our whole lives on it, and many who've come before us have done just that—and lived beautiful, remarkable lives because of it. Not easy or predictable lives by any means, but unforgettable ones, whose ripple effect will be felt for generations to come. Why did the prophets, and the most influential figures in the Bible never give up? Because they lived with that deep, abiding sense of hope. They turned their hearts toward it, again and again, even as doubt and discouragement came knocking on their door. They knew that God will always have the last word, and every struggle, challenge, and circumstance they faced would have to fall in line with that truth eventually. Creation is being redeemed, and it's headed somewhere beautiful, and no one can derail that eternal plan.

Why did you open this book, and what are you hoping to receive from its pages?

When you think about living with more hope in your daily life, what does that look like to you?

Can you recall a time when you felt discouraged or doubtful and God came through for you in a wonderful way?

What is one scripture that brings hope to your heart?

What is one commitment you can make to yourself to help you finish the journey through these pages?

These messages are for you to read in your own way, at your own pace. They might speak to you differently today than they will tomorrow. And whenever you are ready, they are laid out for you in three parts:

Read: Each day, you'll read a reflection that invites you to experience the hope God gives in a new way. It might speak to something you're struggling with right now, or something you may go through in the future, or even something someone you know is facing in their own life. The thoughts and experiences shared here are universal—we all know how heavy doubt, disappointment, and discouragement can feel. So, as we walk our own path, we might find ways to help one another along the journey. The more support we can share, the better.

Reflect: After reading the daily message, take a few moments to answer the questions that follow. You might discover some things you didn't know about yourself as you write them out. Sometimes we have more answers within us than we realize, but they just need the chance to be heard.

Respond: You can choose how to respond to the thoughts shared in these pages. There will be suggestions for actions that you can take to help bring the message into your daily life, but you're the one who knows best how to make that happen. And most importantly, God may lead you to take action in unique and surprising ways as you hear Him speak to your heart.

Look closely for the fingerprints of God's faithfulness throughout the seasons of your life.

NANCY KAY GRACE

His Unchanging Nature

Nature mirrors the image of our Creator in some powerful, inspiring, and breathtaking ways, as the Bible often reminds us. Psalm 19:1–2 (NLT) declares: "The heavens proclaim the glory of God. The skies display His craftsmanship. Day after day they continue to speak; night after night they make Him known." Just think...we can walk out the door and look at any part of the earth or sky above and see a reflection of the One who spoke it all into existence. And one of the most encouraging reminders that creation offers us is this: *God is dependable*. There are certain things about Him that we can count on, no matter what; they've always been true, and they always will be. Think about the patterns you observe (and maybe even take for granted) in the great outdoors, season after season: At a particular time each year, geese get into those fascinating V's of theirs and fly south; it's just what they do, by deliberate design. And the lovely green leaves that are slowly dying on our favorite trees as the weather turns cold? We don't worry about losing them forever. Their vibrant replacements are already in the works, due to sprout next spring. How about the tide we see going out each day? We know that it'll find its way back in, again and again, just like it has since the beginning of time. See, like those patterns in nature, there's a sense of assurance that comes with the things we know we can always count on in our lives. Just as young children thrive most when they're given some structure to feel safe within, we as God's children thrive when we know we're safe in His constant care. Especially when we're navigating life's most uncertain seasons, His unchanging promises can bring us the steadfast hope we need to see us through.

What are your favorite patterns in nature?

Have you ever sat outside just to experience God's presence through His creation, and is that something you could do for a few minutes today?

Has anything happened in your life that made you feel hesitant to hope or trust again?

What's one way you've learned that God can be trusted to show up for you?

Is there anyone you know who could use some reassurance of their loving Father's constant presence and care?

Respond

Allowing ourselves to hope in God is a whole different ballgame than hoping in anything or anyone else. Most of us have experienced the disappointment of being let down in life by something or someone who couldn't be counted on like we thought. It's disorienting, and it can leave us feeling frustrated, doubtful, and vulnerable. When we experience life's uncertainties, we're reminded once again that there is only One we can count on every time, no matter what. Is He predictable? No. It's part of His nature to be beyond our control or complete comprehension. Is He dependable? *Absolutely*. In His way, in His time, He is always working for the good of those who love Him. Consider setting aside some time to reflect on the promises below, taken from God's Word. (Feel free to add your own if you wish.) Think about how you've seen each one play out in your life or the life of someone you know. Choose one promise that you find most difficult to hold onto. Ask God to help you experience the truth of that promise in a deeper way in the days to come. You might even write it out and place it somewhere you will see it often. Let it serve as a daily reminder that His truth is infinitely greater than any doubt you may have. And whenever you can, allow nature to remind you of His constant presence and steadfast love.

Promise of presence: "Do not fear, for I am with you." Isaiah 41:10 (NIV)
Promise of guidance: "He will make your paths straight." Proverbs 3:6 (NIV)
Promise of comfort: "He heals the brokenhearted." Psalm 147:3 (NIV)
Promise of provision: "My God will meet all your needs." Philippians 4:19 (NIV)
Promise of salvation: "By grace you have been saved, through faith." Ephesians 2:8 (NIV)

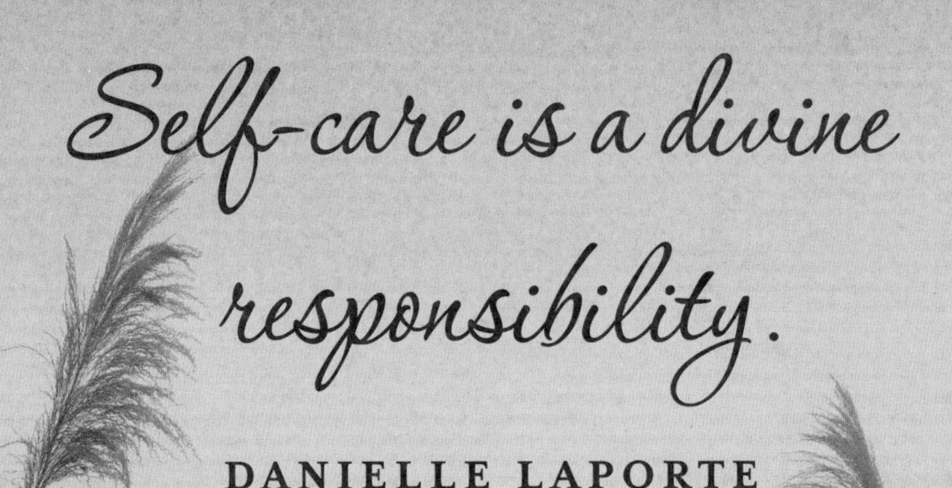

Self-care is a divine responsibility.

DANIELLE LAPORTE

Today's Tune-Up

Are you one of those people who sees a "check engine" light as simply a nice suggestion? Or when that little indicator flashes on, do you drop everything and call the repair shop without delay? And how about your gas gauge? Will you coast into the station on fumes, or does the needle rarely sink below half-tank? Many people fall into one of two general categories when it comes to those kinds of things in our lives: *Proactive* and *reactive*. Some of us just have more laid-back personalities, and others tend to take the bull by the horns. Nothing wrong with either approach, but unfortunately, those of us who fall into the "*re*active" camp often have to learn more things the hard way. That's what happens in our spiritual lives too. We may notice some red flags in our attitude or find ourselves feeling like our love tank is low. People are getting on our nerves; we're quicker to judge and slower to give grace; we notice more discouraging thoughts than grateful ones filling our heads. And if we allow that "struggling spirit" light to stay on *too* long, we can start to feel downright depressed. That's why it's vital for us to maintain our connection with God on the smooth days as well as the rough ones. Instead of waiting until things start going south, we'll surely benefit from checking in from time to time throughout the day, just to feel His presence.

What are some of your spiritual "red flags"—your indicators that it may be time to slow down and fill up?

When was the last time you felt depleted on a soul-deep level, and what did you do about it?

Is there anyone in your life who seems to maintain a healthy balance through their regular connection with God, and what have you learned from them?

Is there anything in your heart that you feel is calling for attention right now?

What's one simple thing you can do today to be proactive in your spiritual life?

Respond

Checking in with ourselves from time to time—really stopping to sense what's going on in our hearts—can be a wonderful practice, and it doesn't have to take long. Here are a few ways anyone can pause for a spiritual tune-up. Remember, being proactive today—however you choose to do so—will make it possible for you to live with more peace and joy tomorrow.

Interviewing: Ask yourself a few questions about how it's been going lately and journal your answers:

- *What's been weighing on my mind and heart, and how can I find more peace about it?*
- *Are any of my relationships in need of some loving attention?*
- *How well have I been caring for myself, and are there any healthy steps I need to take?*

Listening: This is good for anyone who feels drawn to sit quietly in God's presence. Find a favorite place—maybe it's a comfy chair or a spot in the sunshine. Spend a few minutes just being in the midst of all life's doing. Quiet your mind and open your heart for any guidance or reassurance that you might receive.

Reflecting: The Message Bible offers a fresh expression of those familiar fruit-of-the-Spirit verses. Read Galatians 5:22–23 below and consider how you're feeling about what is growing in your own life: "But what happens when we live God's way? He brings gifts into our lives, much the same way that fruit appears in an orchard—things like affection for others, exuberance about life, serenity. We develop a willingness to stick with things, a sense of compassion in the heart, and a conviction that a basic holiness permeates things and people. We find ourselves involved in loyal commitments, not needing to force our way in life, able to marshal and direct our energies wisely."

What a wonderful thought it is that some of the best days of our lives haven't even happened yet.

ANNE FRANK

Happy Endings

Have you ever met someone who likes to read the last line of a book before they even start it? Yes, it's a thing! While that sounds very strange to some of us, it makes perfect sense to others. Those readers want to know what they're getting themselves into, after all. They're about to invest hours of their life in that story, and they like to make sure the payoff in the end is going to be worth it. Plus, they find the whole experience to be less stressful and more fulfilling when they already know whether the villain is going to get away with something, or if those two lovebirds are going to find their way back to each other. So what does this have to do with our spiritual journeys? Well, whether we like spoilers or not, God has already told us where our story is headed...somewhere beyond our wildest dreams. And Jesus promises us in Revelation that He is going to take us there: "I am coming soon" (Revelation 22:12 ESV). No matter what happens between this breath and the last one we take, we can depend on that promise to be our happily-ever-after...and it's no fantasy. As we've all discovered, this story we're living is very real, and not at all easy, but *so* worth it. We can live with hopeful hearts from our first page to our final one on this earth, holding fast to Jesus' promise: "When everything is ready, I will come and get you, so that you will always be with Me where I am" (John 14:3 NLT).

Think of a favorite childhood story with a happy ending. Can you recall that sense of reassurance you felt just knowing it would all turn out okay every time you read it?

Explain how it felt when you first learned the truth about where your journey with Jesus is ultimately headed?

What would your life be like today if you had never learned of God's love for you?

What are you facing right now that could feel less worrisome and more hopeful as you reflect on His eternal promises?

Do you know someone who may need a gentle reminder that what they're going through is only one part of the great story that God is unfolding in their life? How will you remind them today?

Respond

Imagine you've discovered someone who has never heard of Jesus, never read even one of God's promises—someone who looks around at the world today and thinks this is as good as it gets. They believe that when the last chapter of their life on earth is written, that's the end of the story. Period. Now, imagine that you get to be the one to tell them the Good News—that there's Someone who created them and loves them so much that He not only made a way for them to live with joy and peace in *this* life, but He has also prepared a place for them that's beyond what they could ever imagine. Find a pen and some paper and write that person a letter. You could tell them whatever you want to about your life—maybe share what it was like before you met Jesus or heard of God's love. Maybe tell them why you live with hope each day, even when you're going through tough times. The letter can be as simple or as detailed as you wish, but you can write it without holding anything back because it's only for you. Then, try reading those words out loud. Hear your own voice tell the beautiful truth about your life and where it's all going. You'll be reminded in a new way that the personal hope you have in Christ is very real, and that no matter what you're facing today, this story *does* have a happily-ever-after. You've been headed toward it ever since the day God called you to Himself. And *that's* a last page that is definitely worth reading.

God can do anything,
you know—far more than
you could ever imagine
or guess or request
in your wildest dreams!

EPHESIANS 3:20 THE MESSAGE

Life Beyond Limits

What do you think of when you hear the word *limitless*? Maybe the vast, deep blue ocean, or an endless, star-filled sky? It can be hard for our minds to hold the thought of infinite *anything* when we're so used to inhabiting these limited bodies of ours. We live in a world of boundaries and measurements; it's how we humans coexist and make sense of things on this marvelous planet we call home. We live with limits here, and when it comes to resources, we've discovered that there's only so much of this or that thing to go around—so when it's gone, it's gone! It can be scary when there's a shortage of something; when it seems like everyone's scrambling to get whatever they need, however they can; when the world seems less like a kindergarten classroom (*Everyone, take turns and share!*) and more like a battle zone (*Survival of the fittest!*). Our trust that God will provide all we need can waver, and our mindset can go from abundance to scarcity pretty quickly. As soon as we take our eyes off our Provider and focus more on the provision, things start to head south, because the provision may be limited, but the Provider is limitless. And He designed us in such a way that our satisfaction can only be found in Him. No amount of anything can ever replace that truth. So when we catch ourselves feeling the familiar fear of "not enough" creep up, it's a great reminder to take our eyes once again off the world around us and find hope in the One whose Spirit lives within us.

Can you sense the anxiety in the world around you and see how the focus is often on getting more instead of trusting God? Explain your answer.

How about you? In what areas of your life do you feel a sense of scarcity? Abundance?

Have you ever been through a time when God provided in a way you didn't expect? Explain.

The Message Bible *expresses Matthew 6:31 this way: "What I'm trying to do here is to get you to relax, to not be so preoccupied with* getting, *so you can respond to God's* giving." *What does that mean to you in your life right now?*

What is one thing you feel like you don't have enough of, and what's one small step you could take to let go of your fears about it?

Next time you notice that worry or uncertainty has started clouding your days, consider reading Luke 12:22–34 (aka, the "stop overthinking" verses). As you do so, you might use your imagination to envision yourself sitting with Jesus while He was speaking those words on earth. See Him smile at you reassuringly as He gestures toward the birds of the air and flowers in the field, demonstrating how beautifully the natural world reflects a worry-free existence. Does He expect us to ditch our responsibilities, forget about being productive, and just float carelessly through our days? Of course, we know that's not the case. We're designed to do good and meaningful work; it's satisfying, and it gives us a greater sense of purpose. Plus, the Bible reminds us how important it is for us to provide for ourselves and our families. But in the midst of it all, we have a choice: We can hold all we possess today with a tight fist as we fret about getting more tomorrow, or we can relax more and more into the care of our Maker, being grateful for what we have and trusting that He will provide everything we need when we need it. The truth is, no one will ever have "enough" to feel safe or satisfied in this lifetime. We can experience seasons of greater comfort and prosperity, but it isn't helpful to put our faith and hope into those times, because they will eventually slip away. That's just the nature of things. Our God, however, is here for the long haul. He has an endless supply of what we need to thrive each day, and He's not going anywhere. The more we're able to trust in that, the more freedom and joy we'll live with every day.

We don't need perfect words; we just need open hearts.

ANONYMOUS

More Than Words

Raise your hand if you've ever been at a loss for words when trying to comfort or encourage someone who was going through a hard time. At some point, most of us have found our tongues tied, even though our hearts were wide open, just wishing we knew how to say what someone needed to hear. We can do our very best to try to put ourselves into the shoes of another, but at the end of the day, they are the only ones who are walking that path, and no one else knows exactly how it feels. What matters most in those situations isn't that we find the perfect words but that we simply offer ourselves as vessels of God's love. Imperfect as we are, we show up and share whatever we can, trusting that He will always use our best intentions for good. And here's an important note for those of us who are going through hard times ourselves: When we are on the *receiving* end of that support—let us remember that others are doing the best *they* can to lift us up. They want us to know we're not alone; they want us to feel God's peace amid our struggles; they want to shine a light of hope so we can see that those darker times won't last forever. And if they clam up or stumble over their words, if they say something that feels like sandpaper even though they were going for silk, let's remember where their hearts are and sense God's loving presence even in their effort.

Share a time when you shied away from connecting with someone who was having a tough time.

Can you recall a time when you reached out despite your inhibitions? How did it go?

How do you feel when others offer you comfort and encouragement in your struggles? Are you able to recognize their good intentions regardless of their delivery?

Who in your life has been there for you in a memorable way, and how did that happen?

Is there anyone God may be nudging you toward to share His love with as they walk through a tough time? Who is it and how do you plan to reach out?

Respond

Here's the deal: Words can be tricky, even when we use them with the best intentions. That's a great thing to be aware of when it comes to supporting each other through tough times. Consider these thoughts as you make those future connections:

Before reaching out to lift someone up, take a moment to ask for God's timing and direction. Just a simple prayer can make a big difference: "*Lord, please give me the words and actions this person needs most, right when they are needed*."

If you're not sure what to say or do, be honest. Let the person know that you don't have the words, but you want to show up for them however they need. Offer your presence; sitting silently with someone can bring more peace and strength than we may ever realize. God can do a lot in a quiet space with an open heart: As Paul reminds us, "In the same way, the Spirit helps us in our weakness. We do not know what we ought to pray for, but the Spirit himself intercedes for us." (Romans 8:26 NIV).

And when we are on the receiving end of that support, we can remember that those who reach out have taken the time and found the courage to do so because they care. We can receive their imperfect words through a filter of grace, hearing the intent of their hearts over everything else. We can give thanks to a loving Father who never leaves us alone in those discouraging times. He will always send light in the darkness, and how beautiful that we get to be the messengers who carry it to one another.

Do not worry about tomorrow, for tomorrow will worry about itself.

MATTHEW 6:34 NIV

Rising Higher

Disappointment and discouragement. Just the sound of those two words is enough to make us cringe. And when they come knocking on the doors of our hearts? Well, most of us would rather pretend we're not home...and who could blame us? We all go through those times of feeling defeated in life, and they can't end soon enough. Maybe it happens when we fall short of those high expectations we've set for ourselves, or when we wonder if that dream of ours is ever going to get off the ground, or when we're frustrated that we've missed the mark yet again, or we just can't figure out the key to success in some area we're passionate about. We feel a heaviness in our days, our hope flame flickers, and sometimes we wonder if things are ever going to change for the better. That's when we need to remind ourselves that what we see as a "mistake" or a "failure," God sees very differently. It's not that He *wants* us to miss that mark, of course, but He already knows all the ways He's going to use it for our good and His glory. Our job is to trust Him in that—especially in our most defeated moments. We always have the choice: We can use our energy to beat ourselves up, overthink every misstep we made, sink into shame, or blame someone else, or we can redirect that energy toward trusting the One who has already set new opportunities in motion—the One who's working behind the scenes to grow us through our struggles and to grace us with greater compassion for ourselves and others.

Recall a recent time when you felt deeply disappointed.
What brought it about, and how did you work through it?

Are there any discouraging patterns in your life that you feel ready to break out of? What are they?

When have you noticed God bringing silver linings out of a tough situation,
maybe in hindsight?

What would you say to a frustrated child who can't quite get something right?

Are you able to hear your heavenly Father saying the same kind of thing to you?
What do you hear Him saying?

Here's an illustration of how a life surrendered to God is always moving in a hopeful direction, even when we can't feel it! Find some paper and make a single dot on it. Then, from that dot, draw a circle that begins and ends in the same spot. Trace the circle over, and over again, noticing how you keep coming back to that original dot. It's impossible not to, right? Now, beside it, draw a spiral, allowing your pencil to circle around and around as it gradually climbs higher and higher. Trace that spiral a few times, just like you did the circle, but notice that you never come back to the same exact spot. Your pencil may travel back around, but it is always moving higher. When we deal with repeated disappointment or discouragement in our lives, it can feel like that circle—going around and around and just not getting anywhere. But when we begin to see our journey the way God does, we understand that even if we experience familiar setbacks, we are always rising higher—because He's using every little thing for our good. Maybe we learned something more about ourselves this time around, maybe we connected with someone we wouldn't have known otherwise, maybe we are closer than we think to realizing that dream of ours, but we need to trust His timing. After all, He will only reveal what we're ready for. The bottom line is: With God, there is no dead end, no endless cycle of defeat, no meaningless running on a hamster wheel of life. Once we put our trust in Him, there's only one direction for us to head, and that's the hopeful one.

Do what you can,
with what you've got,
where you are.

THEODORE ROOSEVELT

Counting Down

If you've ever had school kids in your home (or remember being one) you might be familiar with the following words, likely uttered in dramatic fashion: *When will I ever need math in my real life?!* Well, besides those engineers, architects, and astronomers who surely have detailed answers to that question, the rest of us can at least agree on this simple mathematical life lesson: Dealing with big numbers takes much more work than dealing with small ones. Pretty obvious, right? For instance, when we look at the headlines in our daily lives and see the devastation of a natural disaster or a large population of people in need, it can feel really overwhelming to us. Our hearts may break as we watch so many of our fellow human beings struggle; our heads may spin as we wonder what we could possibly do to help. We feel conflicted; we don't want to turn a blind eye, and yet, we don't have the ability or resources to make a significant impact on what we're seeing from afar. But remember, we're looking at big numbers, and that's always going to feel like more than we can handle. So let's start small instead. We can't do something for everyone, but we can always do something for *someone*. We can take that headline about one million people and choose to focus on just one. How that happens will be between us and our Maker. But when we take that prayerful step to offer our resources and abilities back to the One who provided them in the first place, He will gladly use what we have to help us make a difference. And even if that difference is for just one person, it's enough—because every single one of us has infinite worth in God's eyes.

How do you handle daily headlines? Do you feel overwhelmed, try not to pay attention, or fall somewhere in the middle?

What's one thing happening in the world that you wish you could help with somehow?

Can you think of an example in Jesus' life when He chose to focus on one person, even though He was surrounded by many in need? Write it down.

Can you recall a time when you were struggling in your life and someone took the time to notice and help you in some way? Write it down.

Who do you know that has made an impact on a few people in a big way, and how have they done that?

You may have heard the story about an old man standing on a beach after a storm that's just caused thousands of starfish to be washed up and stranded on the shore. The man catches sight of a young boy walking toward him, stooping over with every few steps to reach down for one of those stranded creatures and throw it back into the water so it can live. The man asks the boy why he's bothering to do that when there were so many. "What does it matter?" he says. "There are thousands. You can't really make that much of a difference." And the boy lifts the starfish he's holding and says: "But it matters to this one," as he tosses it back into the sea. What a beautiful illustration of how God values each of us infinitely, and how—even when the numbers seem overwhelming—He calls us to reach out, one by one, to touch the lives of our fellow humans. What does that look like for you today? Maybe it's not a global headline; maybe it's folks in your own city who are struggling with addiction, or homelessness, or a health crisis. Maybe it's foster children or nursing home residents—whatever tugs at your heart, there's a reason for it. And while we may be tempted to give in to discouragement when we look at the numbers; we can also remember that boy on the beach and be motivated by the fact that *every one matters*. Consider spending some time in prayer to ask God how you might bless someone with the unique abilities and resources He's given you. Maybe an answer will be clear right away, or perhaps it'll be revealed in the coming days. Regardless, there's one thing you can always count on: Every soul on this earth matters infinitely to Him, and that includes yours.

You are all children of the light and children of the day.

I THESSALONIANS 5:5

Together We Shine

A popular children's toy in the 1980s involved poking tiny, translucent pegs, one by one, into patterns on black paper. Each peg had an assigned spot, and once they were all added together, a light was flipped on behind the paper to illuminate the colorful image that had been created by the pegs. Kids loved to take their creations into extra dark rooms, because that's when they could really see the luminous picture that had appeared. If you think about it, we are like those single pegs before they come together to make a picture—each of us going about our daily lives, uniquely created human beings sharing this great big planet with nearly eight billion others. As we face life's inevitable changes and challenges along the way, we can sometimes feel very alone in our struggles. But it doesn't take long—whether it be a conversation we overhear, a prayer request from a friend, or someone's brutally honest social media post—to realize that everyone is facing *something* they're hoping to make it through. But not everyone has the hope we have in Christ. When we put our hope in Him, our lives are illuminated in a way that they've never been before. And as others who know Him do the same, their light shines too, and God gathers us to create a beautiful picture for the world to see. It's a beacon for others in hard times—a snapshot of His Kingdom here on Earth. When things feel darkest, that's when He shines brightest through all of us, together. Not just so we can make it through tough things, but so others who don't yet know the depth of His love can see it and desire it and open their hearts to receive it.

Can you remember a difficult time you experienced before you were aware of God's deep love for you? How did it feel different from what you experience today?

When you're struggling with something, how do you remind yourself that you're not alone?

How do you see glimmers of God's Kingdom on earth today?

Do you have a few people you can reach out to who can always remind you of the hope you have in Christ? Who are they?

How does it feel to know you are part of the big, beautiful picture God is creating to help others come to know Him?

Galatians 3:26 reminds us: "For you are all children of God through faith in Christ Jesus" (NLT). We're family, in Spirit. That means, of course, we are individuals with our own struggles and strengths, but we will always share the love of one Father. While there will be different reasons for each of us to seek guidance and reassurance throughout our lives, there will always be one, infinite Source for us to draw from: "The one who is the true light, who gives light to everyone" (John 1:9 NLT). How about you today? When you struggle with something, do you tend to do it alone, or are you able to reach out for support on the journey? And when someone else is walking through a tough time, do you offer your presence and loving attention? Sometimes we don't know what to do—whether it be for ourselves or others, and it leaves us feeling a little (or a lot) in the dark. But the moment our hearts whisper, "Help," our God is there, ready to show us the way. Ask Him today if there are any connections you might make in order to share some mutual support and encouragement. Even if there's nothing epic going on at the moment, just building those life-giving relationships will help to strengthen everyone for the unknown road ahead. Pay attention to the people in your life, and the source of their hope. Draw near to the ones who seek the light of Christ in the dark. You can help each other find your way together as you follow Him. And for those who don't yet know the joy of living in His Kingdom, share a little of that light—however you can—to help them on their way, just like someone once helped you.

Symbols are the language of something invisible spoken in the visible world.

GERTRUD VON LE FORT

Making Meaning

People have used symbols to make meaningful connections for centuries. Whether they represent a shared language or a form of self-expression, symbols are a quick way to get a message across, and these days, we're all for that, because...*the quicker the better!* We communicate without words more than we may realize. We're surrounded by accessories, brand logos, computer apps, and let's not forget that ever-growing world of emojis! And while each of those symbols is created with a specific purpose in mind, they will likely represent something different for each of us as we view them through the lens of our belief systems, our life experiences, and our unique perspectives. Even the sacred symbol of the cross means different things to different followers of Jesus. Of course, it is the shared symbol of our faith in Him, but it can also reflect even more about our personal spiritual journeys. For instance, one person might glance at a cross and immediately be reminded of the day they gave their heart to Him; another might feel gratitude for the specific things He's freed them from; another might feel the sense of belonging they value in being part of God's family; and of course, for many of us, the cross is a powerful symbol of the hope that sustains us through every day of our lives.

What are some things that are being communicated around you without words?

Can you think of any symbols that were meaningful in your family growing up, and have you kept them as a part of your life today? What are they?

When you think of the Bible, what symbols come to mind that God seemed to use to connect with people on a deeper level?

Are you someone who tends to look for deep meaning in everything, or do you feel content with just allowing God to make it obvious if there's something He has to communicate?

Do you have any jewelry or other accessories that symbolize something very special in your life? If so, write them down.

Respond

Think about the symbols you're surrounded by in your life. Which ones mean the most to you? It doesn't have to be something you can hold in your hand, either. For some of us, a certain kind of bird reminds us of a loved one; a tree might make us think of strength and flexibility; the moon glowing with the sun's light symbolizes the way we shine with God's love. The possibilities are endless. How about you? What stories do you carry in your heart about the images you see around you? Focus specifically on hope for a moment. What in your surroundings represents hope to you? Try challenging yourself to think outside the box (maybe even *go* outside) and find a few images that lift your heart and give you the sense that everything's going to be okay, because God's got it. It may take some exploration, or perhaps there's something you can think of that is already part of your story. But whatever you choose, ask God to remind you of it from time to time. It can be one of those sweet and simple ways your heart connects with His in your daily life. You may even wish to keep a little picture of it on your phone or mirror or somewhere you'll pass by often. Sometimes, the things that help sustain us on the journey seem pretty simple, but their purpose in inspiring us to connect with our Maker is immense.

When you arise
in the morning, think of
what a precious privilege
it is to be alive, to breathe,
to think, to enjoy, to love.

MARCUS AURELIUS

Rise and Shine

Jesus reminds us often that what's going on in our hearts is the most important thing of all. No matter what we will face in a day, no matter who may challenge or judge us, no matter how much validation we feel from the world outside...nothing matters more than what's happening within. That's why it makes such a difference to begin each day by turning our attention to our heart center—that place where God is present at any moment to connect with us. As we meet Him there in the silence of our *be*ing (before rushing into all our *do*ing), we take our first step onto a more hopeful, peaceful, grateful path for the day, because the state of our hearts will always determine the way we experience the world. Two people can be confronted with the same challenges and experience them completely differently, and it all comes down to what's going on inside them. The Bible reminds us: "Keep vigilant watch over your heart; *that's* where life starts" (Proverbs 4:23 THE MESSAGE). When we find ourselves feeling down, it's natural for most of us to look around for what may be causing it: relationship clashes, stressful work situations, health issues, global unrest. And while these things are difficult for all of us, the true source of discouragement lies within...in our own hearts. The way we respond to what happens in our lives is always in our power, even if we forget that sometimes. It is a freedom given to us by our Maker, and He's there to remind us of that wonderful gift as often as we need.

What's one tough thing you're facing in your life that you would like to have more hope and peace about?

Can you think of a difficult time you've experienced when you had a strong sense of God's comfort and reassurance within you to help you through? Write about it.

What's the first thing you do when you wake up each morning, and does it help to set a positive tone for the day?

Is there anything new you'd like to incorporate into your morning routine?

Can you challenge yourself to take a few extra moments tomorrow morning before your feet hit the floor, just to sense God's presence within you? If so, how would you go about doing this?

Respond

Mornings can be challenging for a lot of us. Before our eyes even flutter open, we may already feel the demands of the day trying to shake us out of bed and nudge us toward that ever-present to-do list. Finding a few moments to set our hearts on a more peaceful path can make a really big difference. That can be as simple as a deep breath, a smile of gratitude, and a reaffirmation of our trust in God: "*Today is in Your hands*." Those few quiet moments spent with Him may not seem like much, but they're like seeds we plant that can, over time, produce beautiful fruit in our lives.

Here are a few questions you can ask yourself at the start of the day (or just every once in a while) to help you tune into your heart and lean into your Maker:

- *How do I feel about this day?*
- *Are there any "clouds" hanging over my head, and if so, why?*
- *What is happening in my heart that may be causing this heaviness?*
- *What are a few ways I can free myself to feel differently today?*

Ask God to help you become more aware of what's happening within you; allow Him to reveal any negative thoughts or attitudes you need to let go of. Envision yourself moving through the day with a sense of hope and gratitude. And if outward circumstances threaten to shake things up, just take a deep breath and return to your heart center, where you'll always find God's Spirit offering you His peace.

Be patient.
The best things
happen unexpectedly.

ANONYMOUS

Shaking It Up

Is there anyone in your life whose timeline has looked very different than what's often considered "normal" or expected in our culture? For instance, maybe they were just beginning their dream job when others their age were retiring; or when their peers were settling down to start families, they were just beginning to explore the world; or perhaps they suddenly discovered an ability they had that changed the course of their life. There are so many examples of people who've taken unexpected detours and achieved unlikely goals, it's a wonder we limit anyone with our expectations. We tend to gravitate toward what's familiar in life because it feels safer. So when people surprise us by pushing boundaries and choosing unexpected paths, it can be a wonderful wake-up call. They remind us that nothing is set in stone—that every day brings possibilities we could never have predicted. If we want to live the most purposeful and fulfilling lives imaginable, then we have to stop limiting ourselves to business-as-usual. God will always have more for us, but we have to be open to receiving it. Should we assume that just because most of our friends went to college twenty years ago, it's probably not going to happen for us? Or if we're hoping to find a partner in life and it doesn't seem to be working out, that we've likely missed the boat? Or how about that thing we just *know* we've been called to do, but none of the pieces are coming together...*what's up with that?* Should we just give up? Our tiny human expectations pale in comparison to the limitless possibilities God holds for our lives. The more we let go of the timelines we cling to, the more space we have for Him to work.

Is there anything in your life that you feel you've waited on for so long, you've lost hope about it? What is it?

What's something unpredictable that has happened to you, that you could see God's hand in?

Write about someone whose story took a turn for the better, maybe when they least expected.

Does the idea of letting go of expectations bring you a sense of fear or relief? And why do you think that is?

Is there anything in your life that you've hesitated to try because it might be considered unusual for your family, culture, or age group? What is it?

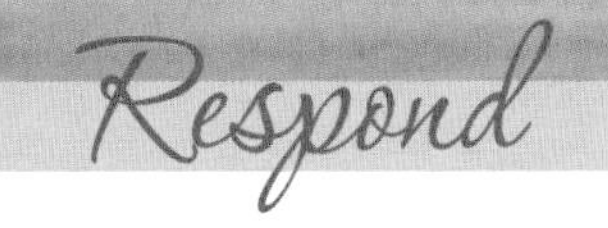

Spend some time online, at the library, or among your circle of family and friends to learn about people who have done unexpected things at unforeseen times in their lives. Maybe the ones who've taken detours in their later years, or those whose unlikely abilities and accomplishments have surprised the world around them. Why is it important to pay attention to these things? Because when we find ourselves feeling "stuck" or we have that "never-gonna-happen" feeling weighing us down, we can remember that *no one knows* like God knows. He can take what looks like a dead end to us and turn it into a new beginning in an instant. He can take our average expectations and blow them clean out of the water with something we never even dreamed of. Centuries ago, a man named Job poured every ounce of His faith into God, trusting Him to show up at a time of deep uncertainty: "I know that you can do all things; no purpose of yours can be thwarted" (Job 42:2 NIV). He goes on to acknowledge that human tendency we all have: "Surely I spoke of things I did not understand, things too wonderful for me to know" (Job 42:3 NIV). And that's the heart of the matter for all of us: There are things ahead on our journeys too wonderful for us to know. There are things we think we *want* that God will replace with what He knows we *need* in order to experience the most fulfilling lives imaginable. Our job is to let go (again and again) and trust His process.

Faith goes up the stairs that love has built and looks out the windows which hope has opened.

CHARLES SPURGEON

Living Hope

Have you ever heard the theory that the five closest people in your life have the greatest effect on your well-being? Supposedly, it's those few people we most commonly interact with who have the strongest influence on our behavior and our attitudes—which makes sense. Of course, there are many factors that play into how we show up in our lives (most significantly, our relationship with God) but it's hard to deny that we are influenced, at least a little, by those we surround ourselves with. We are relational beings after all, and the people with whom we have significant connections are going to affect us in one way or another. Think about those you spend the most time around (not counting toddlers and teens). Whom do you interact with regularly, and how does it make you feel to be in their presence? Can you name one or more truly positive people in your life—people who choose to look at the bright side and inspire you to do the same? It's nearly impossible to spend time around an uplifting person without feeling a little lighter, a little more hopeful. It's as if these people have an essence of hope living within them, like a tune without words. Those people in our lives who carry that upbeat tune are true blessings, and we, in turn, have the opportunity to pass that gift along to others.

Do you see yourself as a generally hopeful person — why, or why not?

Think of the most positive person and the most negative person in your life and describe how you feel around each of them.

Do you have any relationships that weigh you down, and have you considered praying for guidance in those connections?

Do you have any acquaintances you'd like to get to know better based on their positive influence in your life? Who are they?

What's one thing you could do today to move the needle in your life a little more toward hope?

Respond

In Paul's Spirit-filled pep talk to the Thessalonians, he reminds them to, "Rejoice always, pray continually, give thanks in all circumstances" (I Thessalonians 5:16–18 NIV). Sure, it's a pretty high bar to set for the rest of us, but we can always see it as a helpful direction to head in, rather than some sort of perfection to achieve. As we allow praise, prayer, and gratitude to become more evident in our lives over time, it will not only affect us, but the people around us too. A truly joyful heart cannot help but spill over into others, and by God's design, that will create a ripple effect that reaches further than we may ever know. Here's a little tune-up we can give our hearts anytime, anywhere, and it only takes a few moments. We can ask ourselves these three questions, based on Paul's words:

- *What's one reason I have to rejoice in God today?*
- *Whom or what can I lift up in prayer in this moment?*
- *What's one new thing I am thankful for?*

It's that simple. Praise. Pray. Give thanks. And just like every other habit we form, when we do it consistently, we will find that it starts to shape us in new ways. One day, we will look back and see what a difference those few moments a day have made in the bigger picture of our lives. As we start to carry a soul-deep sense of hope, we will naturally fulfill the call to "encourage one another and build each other up" (I Thessalonians 5:11 NIV) not just because it's something we *do* all the time, but because it's who we *are*.

It's not what you look at that matters. It's what you see.

HENRY DAVID THOREAU

The View from Above

At some point in life, many of us—regardless of how strong our faith is, how much we've grown, or how successful our endeavors have been—still ask ourselves things like: *Is my life really going anywhere? Does it mean anything? What kind of lasting difference have I made in the world?* Yes, even followers of Jesus. Even those who know that our ultimate significance lies in the fact that we are God's beloved children, regardless of what we've accomplished, we still have that desire to know not just *that* we matter...but *how* we matter. We look at the string of days behind us and try to see how they might reveal a life well-lived. And as we do so, we're likely to find some great things—some wonderful accomplishments and right decisions and life-giving relationships we've built. But we may also find some moments we're not so proud of—some unfinished business, hurtful interactions, and frankly, a few paths we just wish we hadn't taken. That's when it is helpful to zoom out a bit and see the bigger picture. Think of looking out the window of an airplane. The higher you get, the more you see how everything is connected—tiny squares of land interwoven by threads of winding roads. It's a patchwork quilt of farms and cities, rivers and mountains, coexisting meaningfully with one another. And if you could take out one of those patches, it would be like a missing puzzle piece, affecting everything around it. That's exactly how it is with our lives: Every part has significance as the past, present, and future are being woven together into God's beautiful purpose for us. It all matters in the end.

What's one thing about your past that you've had a hard time letting go of?

What's one thing you struggle to understand about your life today?

What's one thing you fear about the future?

Is there anyone you know who encourages you to find a bigger-picture perspective when you're feeling discouraged about life or down on yourself? Who is it?

How can the promise, "Jesus Christ is the same yesterday and today and forever" (Hebrews 13:8 NIV) bring you peace and assurance as you consider your answers above?

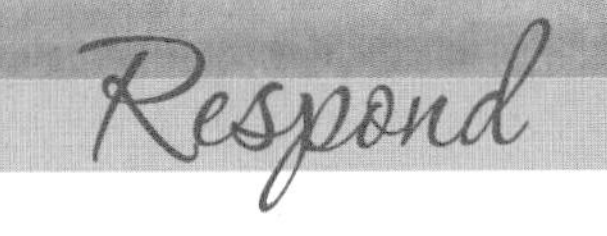

When we're feeling discouraged about our purpose or plan in life, drawing closer to our heavenly Father can help us see things in a clearer, more meaningful way. Think about it like this: Say you have a friend standing several feet away from you with her phone held up, ready to snap a picture of something that you can't quite see. You're curious about what she's viewing through that lens, but you know that the only way to see what she's seeing is to move closer to her. That's an illustration of how God invites us to lean into Him as we look at our own lives. If we want to get a better idea of how He sees things, we can draw close to Him anytime and ask for help with our perspective. Of course, we know it doesn't mean we'll have answers to all the "whys," or suddenly comprehend the intricate web of connections we're involved in, but it *does* mean that we will have more peace about how it's all coming together for our highest good. Think about the questions you answered on the previous page as you reflected on the timeline of your life. Spend some time in prayer asking if there's anything God has for you to see about those past situations, your current circumstances, or future fears. Ask Him, most of all, to fill you with a sense of reassurance that—even when you can't see how—He is weaving it all together for your good. The more you're able to surrender to that truth, the more you can enjoy this moment for what it is and trust that the rest will always be in His hands.

If we don't change,
we don't grow.
If we don't grow,
we aren't really living.

GAIL SHEEHY

Feeling the Burn

Do you have any of those candles around your house that have never been lit? Maybe they're fancy-looking and ornate or they match your decor perfectly, and you don't want to burn them down...so you just leave them out to look pretty? It's a funny thing about candles; when they're doing what they're made to do, they don't keep that lovely facade for long. They burn and soften and change shape, disappearing slowly, sometimes ending in a lumpy heap. Sure, the flame is lovely to look at, but that wax underneath? It's going through quite a meltdown. If you think about it, we humans often see ourselves like those untouched candles. We have this expectation that our lives aren't supposed to get messy or change form. Things aren't supposed to get uncomfortable or to hurt, and when they do, there's *surely* something wrong with us. We may believe we've gotten off-track somewhere, and the ideal life we're striving for seems to be disappearing before our eyes. But the truth is, our Maker didn't create us to sit on a shelf looking pretty, collecting dust. He knew way before we showed up for our brief stay on this marvelous planet that we would face challenges and that our lives would change form many times. He knew that as we surrendered our old lives in order to become more and more like Christ, those "selves" we tried to create without Him would gradually disappear in order for something real and eternal to take shape in us. This is why, when we're feeling the "burn" of the most difficult things, we must remind ourselves that it all has purpose. Even if it wasn't intended by God, it's all being used by Him for good, and not one drop of it will be wasted.

Do you have expectations of what your life "should" look like right now, and how are you feeling about it?

Can you recall a time when something difficult happened that ended up helping you grow in a big way? Write about it.

Think about the challenges you face. Do you feel instantly discouraged and focused on the negative, or do you naturally try to look for silver linings?

How can you remind yourself to keep God's big picture in mind on extra rough days?

What's one bit of biblical truth that can bring you some light when you feel discouraged or disappointed?

Spend some time in prayer and reflection, thinking back to some of the hardest seasons in your life. Recall the hopelessness you may have felt or the sense of disappointment that things had not turned out as you wanted them to. Now, ask God to remind you of the ways He worked in those situations: maybe through the support of someone who showed up for you or a resource that brought you some comfort or even a healthy distraction to help you through a rough patch. Even if you can't think of one silver lining, you can simply be grateful that you survived whatever it was, and that you know that He had a hand in it. And now here you are, reading these words, being reassured that He has never—and will never—leave your side, even when you can't sense His presence in the way you might expect. Whatever you are going through today, God stands ready to provide the comfort and reassurance you need. Consider reading the stories of His people throughout history—Moses, Joseph, David, and many others—who had to trust that their heavenly Father had allowed their challenges for reasons that they could not yet understand. But in that trust, they found freedom, right in the middle of the mess of life...and we can too. Just remember, you are never alone when you're feeling the "burn." We are all learning to let go of our idea of what our lives are supposed to look like so that our Maker can shape us into the beautiful creations He already sees when He looks at us today.

Never be limited by other people's limited imaginations.

DR. MAE JEMISON

Thinking Bigger

In the 1500s, the term *pigeonhole* was first used to describe a tiny place within a large coop of birds where pigeons were put to nest. Today, of course, we use that term to describe what happens when people think "small" about one another—when we make very narrow assumptions about each other without first considering all the qualities or characteristics someone might possess. Unfortunately, this happens more than we realize. It's not that we intentionally *try* to underestimate the potential or worth of another person; in fact, we may not be conscious of it. But it's been happening for humans, in one way or another, since the beginning of time. It shouldn't surprise any of us to know that Jesus was not a "pigeonholer," in any way. He looked at the high and mighty Pharisee the same way He looked at the down-and-out person on the street. He did not allow their culture, class, status, or any other category that the world used to define them, to limit His belief in their potential. Sure, He had some brutally honest words for those self-righteous fellows who thought they were all that...*but* He didn't say those things out of spite. He said them with some tough love. He was always inviting people into freedom with His words, challenging them to see that—as God's creations—they were more than they ever realized. And of course, the same is true for us today. When we keep our minds and hearts open for one another, we are following in His footsteps. And when *we're* the ones who feel undervalued or underestimated, we need to remember that our worth is determined by God alone...and that worth is infinite.

How do you see people in the world making narrow assumptions about each other, and what kind of toll has it taken?

Is there anyone you know who feels limited by others' beliefs or opinions about them, and how might you encourage them?

Who in your life sees your potential, supports your growth, and helps you remember your worth?

What's one thing you feel you've doubted about yourself due to other people underestimating or making assumptions about you?

Who's an underdog in the Bible who inspires you?
Someone who did what no one thought they could do?

Respond

Here are two questions we can ask ourselves that can help us live free of those limiting beliefs:

1. How do I tend to think small about others—even unintentionally?

Spend a few moments reflecting on how you perceive your fellow humans—not only those with whom you share close relationships, but the people "out there" in the world. Whether it be a friend, a neighbor, that guy who posts constantly on social media, or the actress you've never met. Are there certain people you've formed opinions or made judgments about, and can you see how those limitations really are unnecessary, and can even be hurtful? If that resonates with you, ask God to help you hold more space and grace for other human beings, acknowledging that He is the only One who truly knows each of us inside and out.

2. How does it affect me when others think small about me?

Whether or not you're aware of it, there will always be people in your life who have opinions about what kind of person you are and what you're capable of. This is hard to hear for many of us because we just wish others would mind their own business and let us do our thing! But since we can't control anyone else's thoughts, we can turn our energy instead toward ourselves. We can root ourselves more strongly than ever in God's truth about who we are because, in the end, that's the only truth that makes a difference anyway! Don't shrink to fit anyone's narrow assumptions about you; always see yourself growing in Christ. He is the One who determines the possibilities for your life, and no human can come close to understanding you the way He can.

You cannot protect yourself from sadness without protecting yourself from happiness.

JONATHAN SAFRAN FOER

Feeling It All

Grief is something many of us don't like to talk about, and it's *definitely* something we wish we didn't have to experience. We all know that it doesn't only show up when someone we love dies; it's a natural process we go through for many reasons in our lives: the necessary end of a friendship, letting go of our attachment to something we've held dear, having to move away and leave a place behind where we've made so many memories. There are all kinds of "surrenders" for us to experience in this life, but there is one hopeful thing they all share in common: *The grief we allow ourselves to feel today will become fertile ground for joy tomorrow.* That can be hard to believe while we're in the midst of it, but when we look back one day, we will surely see how true it is. Our loving Creator knew from the beginning that all our letting go would make room for new life in our hearts. As we feel the sadness of loss, we also honor and deeply appreciate those gifts we were given, no matter how long we were able to enjoy them. As we draw close to God and witness His tender heart toward us, we become vessels of compassion for ourselves and for others. The more honest we are about our feelings, allowing ourselves to move through them, the lighter we will be on the other side, because we will no longer be carrying something we were always meant to lay down. Jesus knew what it was to grieve—not only during that oft-quoted time when He wept at the loss of His friend, Lazarus, but all the "letting go's" that He surely had to do as a human on this earth. We can find hope and take comfort in the fact that He knows exactly how to lead us through our own times of loss.

How do you cope when sadness shows up in your heart? Do you slow down and allow yourself to feel it, or do you tend to try to ignore it?

Is there a loss in your life that you can look back on and see the healing that has taken place in you since? Write about it.

Describe a time when you experienced the truth of Psalm 34:18 (NIV)? "The Lord is close to the brokenhearted and saves those who are crushed in spirit."

Do you think it's true that people who try to avoid feeling the hard things are limited in their capacity to feel deep joy? Why or why not?

Is there anyone in your life today who could use a word of comfort as they are letting go of something or someone? If so, write the words you want to say to them below.

Respond

Here's an experiment that can illustrate how important it is for us to feel the things we need to feel. Wherever you are right now, take a deep breath and hold it in as long as you can. You'll know when it gets uncomfortable enough to let it out. While you're holding that breath though, feel what happens in your body. You'll probably tense up a bit; your mind will start wondering when you're going to feel some relief; you may even get a little anxious. That's what can happen on a heart level when we try to stuff down our sadness for too long. We may not even realize it, but those unexpressed feelings can cause a lot of unrest within us. Now, take some long, slow, deep breaths. Feel how they bring a sense of calm throughout your body. This is what can happen when we let our feelings flow. Since we're often unaware of the extra weight we sometimes carry in our hearts, it's good to ask God once in a while to reveal anything we might need to let go of in order to make room for more hope and joy. It may surprise us to discover that there are losses in our lives that we never really took the time (or felt like we had the permission) to grieve. Please remember this...there's no set timetable for healing. When we discover that we're carrying something we don't want to anymore and we're ready to experience greater freedom within, we can always count on a loving Father who stands ready to take our hand and walk us through it. The first step is simply to ask; then we keep our hearts open for Him to show us the way.

All we have to decide
is what to do with
the time that is given us.

J.R.R. TOLKIEN

Deep Time

Many of us grew up hearing sayings like "a watched clock never ticks" or "a watched pot never boils," when we were hyper-focused on something we just *could not wait one more minute for!* It's a tendency many of us share: we set these expectations, and until they're met (preferably sooner than later), we're not going to be truly happy and satisfied. We're just going to be...*waiting*. There are so many other things going on around us, but those things don't matter so much because they're not what we've been hoping for. And as we set our laser focus on what we want, as we tap our feet with impatience, anticipating that *ding!* or delivery or reward or whatever else our instantly gratified world has convinced us we need right now...we often miss something much more important. We miss what God has for us in this moment, right here. Let's be clear, though: there's nothing wrong with anticipation. It's all part of the journey! God created us with the capacity for hope, and how wonderful that we get to experience that inner knowing that good things are on their way in our lives. But as we look forward to those things, let us never forget where our feet are *right now*. This is the only moment that truly matters because (as you may have noticed) we never do reach that future. Tomorrow always becomes today. We simply live through one long string of present moments, from our first breath to our last. That clock will tick, whether we are watching it or not, but we will enjoy the whole experience of life so much more if we leave the timing to God and turn our awareness toward *what is*...here and now.

Describe a time you were so keenly focused on something you were waiting on that you realized you were missing the joy of the moment.

Is there anything you can think of right now that may be keeping some of your happiness "on hold" while you wait for its arrival? If so, what is it?

Is there anyone in your life who seems to be more focused on the future than the present, and what do you notice about them?

Is there anyone you know who just seems to be more present in life, and how do they inspire you?

What's one thing you could do when you catch yourself "watching the clock" to remind yourself to come back to the moment?

Second Peter 3:8 (NIV) offers us a lovely reminder about the time outside of time where God dwells: "But do not forget this one thing, dear friends: With the Lord a day is like a thousand years, and a thousand years are like a day." The Bible reminds us often that our earthly ways of measuring things can be very different from God's. We may be counting the minutes or days until some kind of "arrival," but meanwhile, our Creator is offering us a much fuller, more immediate experience of life that isn't dependent on the ticking hands of a clock. He invites us to live fully and contentedly, right where we are, even as we wait for future things. You may have heard of those two distinct words the ancient Greeks used to refer to time: *chronos* and *kairos*. *Chronos* is most familiar to us; it's linear, measurable, all about quantity. But *kairos*... that's something altogether different. Some people call it "deep time"—those moments when everything else just seems to stop, and we simply feel the joy of being alive. Here's a challenge for you: Start paying attention to what's pulling you out of the present. Whether it's checking your phone, anticipating an arrival of some kind, or even fantasizing about how wonderful life will be *as soon as*... (fill in the blank). When you notice that you're up in your head, missing what's right in front of you, just take a deep breath, return to the moment with grateful awareness and say, "Thank You, Lord, for *what is*, right now." Even if it only happens once a day, over time this simple practice can help you become more aware of the blessings that surround you in the present, even as you anticipate all the good the future can bring.

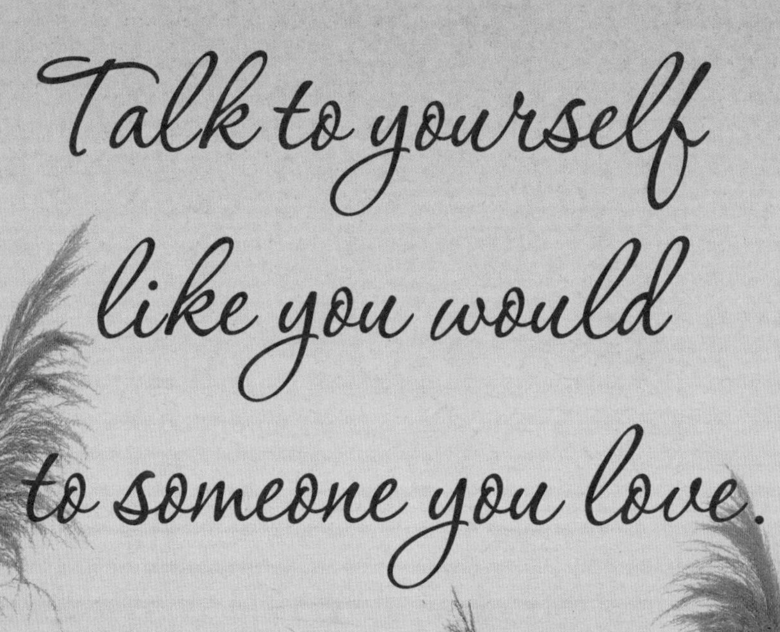

Talk to yourself like you would to someone you love.

BRENÉ BROWN

Dear Me

When we were kids, we did a lot of waiting for someone bigger to help us with those things we weren't grown enough to do—things like reaching high shelves, driving us to baseball games, or making us our favorite grilled cheese. But more significantly, we often looked to those grown-ups to tell us they were proud of what we did, to encourage us when we were down and out, to check under the bed for monsters and reassure us that there were none. If we had the blessing of loving caregivers in our lives, we knew there was someone we could count on to say the words we most needed to hear. Fast-forward to adulthood, and here we are, needing to hear some of those same things: *It's going to be okay. You're safe. You're loved. You matter. You're not alone.* And it's wonderful when we have family, friends, church communities, and other folks in our lives who can remind us of those truths. But here's the kicker: There's no guarantee that the words of encouragement, affirmation, or reassurance that we're waiting for are going to come from outside of us. If we wait until they do, we're putting our sense of well-being into the hands of someone else. And that's not how we were designed to live our best lives. God has given us the wonderful ability to speak to our own hearts—to tell ourselves the truth we need to hear in any situation, and to allow it to bring us the peace, hope, and joy that is always available to us in Him. We must never forget that one powerful way His love comes to us is *through* us.

As a child, did you have a caregiver who gave you the encouragement and reassurance you needed? Write about that experience.

What words are you speaking to yourself today?

Is there any way you feel you've put your sense of happiness and well-being into the hands of someone else, hoping they will validate or affirm you in some way? If so, describe the situation below.

Do you enjoy your own company, or do you look for distractions to avoid being alone with yourself? Explain.

What are your thoughts about God loving you through you? Does that seem like a strange idea or something you have experienced?

Respond

What do you need to hear right now in your life? How about when you first wake up in the morning? Or when you feel beat down? Or when you are wondering how that situation or relationship is ever going to work out? Do you need hope? Comfort? Motivation? A reminder that you're enough, in this moment, exactly as you are? Just pretend for today that nothing you need to hear is going to come from outside yourself. Any words your heart longs to receive are up to *you* to provide. And you're going to do it (if you choose to participate) in a letter to yourself. Write "Dear Me" at the top of your journal page, paper, or computer screen. Take a deep breath, close your eyes, and ask yourself what words you most need to hear right now. Be aware of God's loving presence with you and ask Him to show you how you may be waiting for someone else to validate you or encourage you or just let you know it's all going to be okay. Allow yourself to witness those places within that feel empty and are needing to be filled. Maybe even see yourself as a child, leaning into Jesus, feeling His arms of love and protection around you. And when you're ready, tell that child in you everything they've been waiting to hear. You might read what you write out loud to yourself and let that wonderful truth sink in. Or tuck it away in a place where you can pull it out when you need it most. In the days ahead, you might become even more aware of the ways you wait for things to come from outside yourself. When you notice that happening, gently remind yourself that God has already provided all you need within.

The best way to find out what we really need is to get rid of what we don't.

MARIE KONDO

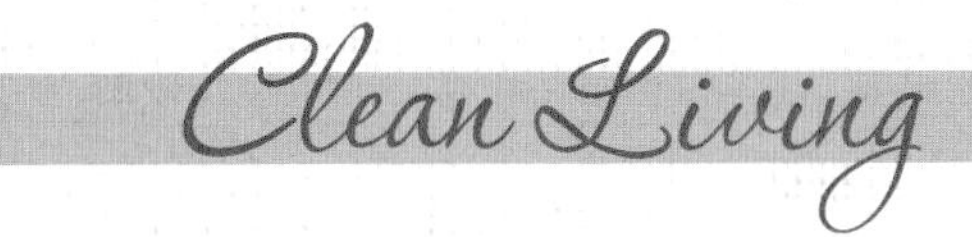

Clean Living

Spring cleaning is a practice many of us are familiar with—maybe it's something our grandparents or parents did, or we might even do it ourselves each year. It's that centuries-old tradition of a deep house cleaning that ushers out the long winter months and welcomes the newness of spring. There's something so refreshing and hopeful about getting to open the windows and air things out, and it can be surprising when we discover what's been lurking in corners and on windowsills for far too long. While we're clearly talking about a physical activity here, it can also illustrate the importance of another kind of practice—a spiritual one. It can be so helpful for us to set aside a significant time (doesn't have to be just once a year, either) to do a little housecleaning in our hearts. Because many of us live full lives in a fast-paced culture, we can get so busy checking off our to-do lists and covering our bases that we lose touch with what's happening within us. What attitudes have we picked up? What regrets are we dragging along? What worries have been collecting in our lives for so long, we forget how it feels to live free of them? "Spiritual spring cleaning" can be a game changer, and we can do it during any season of our lives!

How has life felt for you lately? Have you been waking up on the "sunny side" or dreading the days, and what do you think is affecting how you feel?

What's one thing you've struggled with in the past that your heart is free of today?

Is there anything you know you've been holding on to that you'd like to be free of?

How did Jesus inspire people to live more authentically by looking within themselves?

Imagine that your heart is a home—are the rooms mostly free of clutter, or does it need some loving attention? Explain.

Jesus was a Master at revealing the hidden things—the well-disguised motives, unexpressed hurts, and self-deceit people carried, often unknowingly. He knew that the longer we go without clearing out those things that don't belong to us, the more discouragement and despair we will live with—even if we aren't aware of where it's coming from. That's why one of the greatest gifts we can give ourselves is a deeper look within. We can ask our loving Father to open those doors within our hearts and help us discover what's hiding there—what needs healing and confessing. Just becoming aware of those things is a big step. Like those dust bunnies gathered under our beds, we don't even know to reach for them if we don't realize they're living there in the first place. So whether you've been feeling wonderful or wary about life lately, consider taking some time in a quiet place to do these three things:

1. *Ask God to reveal anything that's weighing you down.*
2. *Spend some time prayerfully listening and write down anything that comes to your mind and heart.*
3. *Commit to taking one step to address whatever comes up, however that may look for you.*

Pay attention to how God works in the coming days to help you clean up that clutter and live more freely and joyfully. This can be a wonderful tradition to establish, and just like that spring cleaning practice, it'll surely bring a greater sense of hope and lightness to the home that is your heart.

All the darkness
in the world
cannot extinguish
the light of a
single candle.

FRANCIS OF ASSISI

Finding Freedom

Those of us who've been on this planet for any amount of time have learned that there are many things we cannot control...and only a few precious things that we can. This isn't usually what we want to hear, but the sooner we learn to accept the truth of it, the more peaceful our lives can become. Not because our circumstances change, of course, but because we surrender to the fact that, as someone once so wisely stated: "There is a God, and He is not us." (Thank heaven!) As we learn to use *less* energy trying to manage what isn't in our job description as human beings, we free up *more* energy for what we are actually here to do: Serving God and one another in love. This is especially important to remember during discouraging times in life. Maybe we can't do a whole lot to change our conditions at the moment, but that's okay. Because there will always be a few things we *can* do—even small things—and the sooner we focus on those, the more hopeful we will feel. The movie, *La Vita e Bella (Life Is Beautiful)* is a moving example of finding glimmers of hope in a dire situation. It's the story of Guido Orefice, a gentle Jewish-Italian father, and his son imprisoned in a 1930s concentration camp. Guido chooses to focus on brightening his little boy's life in the midst of what many of us imagine to have been a hopeless existence. He finds creative ways to lift spirits and lighten hearts. And while we may never face that degree of heaviness in our lives, we can take a lesson from his valiant effort: We can always find ways to bring a sense of hope to our environment. Sometimes it just takes a little creative vision.

Recall a time when you found yourself in challenging circumstances that were out of your control. How did you handle it?

What advice would you give a loved one going through a time like that today?

Is there anyone you know (including yourself) who is facing challenges right now, and what simple thing could you do to shine the light of hope into that situation?

Who in your life (or anywhere in the world) has a story that inspires you to find ways to thrive despite your limitations?

Write out a verse that you can share with a friend who needs encouragement.

When we find ourselves in tough situations that are out of our control, we may feel fearful, trapped, resentful, and sometimes even hopeless. It can be hard to stop our heads from spinning and our hearts from hurting as we wonder why it's happening and how we're ever going to get through it. We value our freedom as human beings, and when we feel like parts of it are taken away unfairly, we struggle mightily to accept that. Whether or not you're dealing with an experience like this right now, there is something you can consider doing anytime you're feeling boxed in by life: *Use your imagination*. It can help you shift your focus from *What can't I do?* to *What's possible for me right now?* Perhaps you're separated from someone you love for a while. And while you miss them more than you can say, there's nothing you can do to change it at the moment. So you decide to put your energy toward nurturing a friendship that brings joy to your heart. Of course, it doesn't make things "all better," but it *can* bring some lightness to your life. Or maybe you aren't able to use your body to dance right now due to a physical limitation. Why not focus on those things you still *can* do that make your heart happy? If you want to find other ways to enjoy music, consider learning an instrument. Or teach a child a song from when you were little. Focus less on what you can't do and more on what you *can*. See how it feels to live more and more from that perspective. We don't often understand why God allows us to experience these tough times, but we never have to question whether He's there in the midst of them, offering us new ways to find joy in Him, regardless of our circumstances.

Courage doesn't always roar. Sometimes courage is the little voice at the end of the day that says I'll try again tomorrow.

MARY ANNE RADMACHER

Meeting Your Fears

When you think back on your childhood, you probably remember at least a few significant times when you felt very afraid. And from your adult perspective, some of those times may now seem a little "silly." Monsters under the bed, sharks in the swimming pool, something lurking in the attic...you get the idea. And even if you can't remember back that far, there may be children in your life right now who can remind you as they face their own fears of the dark. Fear is fear, after all—at any age, from any perspective. We may all experience it for different reasons, but we all know how it feels. And no matter what stage of life we're in or what we're feeling afraid of, it's so helpful to meet ourselves with the kind of compassion Jesus has for us. Think about what happens when a child cries out in the night. A loving parent often responds by offering their presence. Instead of shaming that little one or dismissing their fear and telling them to just "get over it," the parent tries to understand where it's coming from. They may ask, "What happened to make you feel afraid?" And once their child has shared what's on their mind, he or she may be offered a few minutes in the rocking chair or something else to help them feel a sense of safety and reassurance. Now: fast forward to adulthood. It's highly unlikely that someone is waiting in the other room to soothe us after a nightmare anymore. But we still have a loving Father who assures us wholeheartedly: "I am the LORD your God who takes hold of your right hand and says to you, Do not fear; I will help you" (Isaiah 41:13 NIV). How well do we sense His presence when we need it most?

Reflect

What were some of your biggest childhood fears?

What are some of your greatest fears today?

When you find yourself feeling afraid, how do you tend to handle it?

Have you ever felt dismissed by someone who didn't understand how scared you were in a situation, and what was that like for you?

When you know that someone in your life is feeling afraid about something, how do you reassure them?

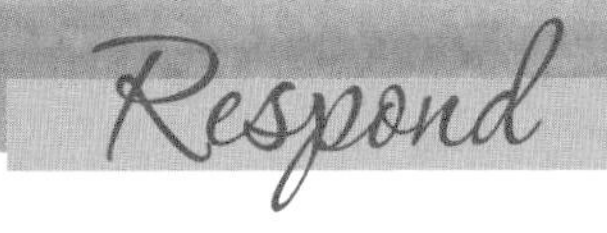

Unlike that loving parent described in today's devotion, we're often quite hard on ourselves when it comes to dealing with difficult emotions. We may feel embarrassed or frustrated that we can't just "get over" something. Maybe the monster under our bed has to do with feeling inadequate in our work, expecting the worst with a health diagnosis, being worried about finances...the list goes on. Just because we deal with "grown-up" issues these days, doesn't mean we feel any more confident than we did as children. We still need to be met with tenderness and understanding. We still need reassurance and reminders that everything's going to be okay. And the good news is, the Source of all those wonderful things lives within us. God's Spirit offers us all we need to feel safe and secure in His love. His presence is constant, but the tricky part is getting ourselves to stop and listen long enough to be aware of it. Next time you discover those uninvited worries or fears knocking on your door, try to catch yourself before you start down the path of "*Why can't I just get over this?*" or "*How can I get away from this awful feeling?*" Instead of stuffing it down or scurrying to manage it, take a moment to sit with it. Close your eyes, take a deep breath, and acknowledge God's presence calming you like the most patient, understanding, compassionate Father in the universe (because He is, you know). Acknowledge what you're feeling, and trust that there's a message for you in it. Ask if there's anything you need to see about the root of that fear, and then thank Him for walking so closely with you through everything. The more you do this, the more naturally you will be able to walk in peace, no matter what life brings.

Patience is the calm acceptance that things can happen in a different order than the one you have in mind.

DAVID G. ALLEN

The Art of Waiting

What does your patience meter look like these days? Are you one of those people who keeps opening the oven to check the cookies when you know full well they're not done? Maybe you scoot them around a bit and stare real hard, hoping that somehow, they'll turn that perfect golden-brown color right before your eyes. Sure, the timer says ten more minutes, but your sweet tooth says...*now!* Or maybe you're the kind of person who can just let it go and walk away. Those cookies will be done when they're done, and no amount of peeking in is going to change that. When it comes to having patience in our lives, most of us are somewhere in the middle, depending on the situation or season we're in. Sometimes, we're able to take that age-old "let go and let God" advice and let it be. Other times, we're white-knuckling everything, determined to make it all work our way and in our time. And while checking on cookies doesn't have a significant effect on us, trusting God's timing in the bigger things does. It can be really hard to admit that we don't have much control over our circumstances. That doesn't mean we're helpless, of course; it just means we're not running the universe, and we do much better in the back seat than we would at the helm. And when we learn to strive less and surrender more, we can find true joy in being along for the ride.

How patient do you feel you are, in general?

Can you think of a recent situation when you had a "checking the cookies" mentality, and how did it work out for you?

Now, how about a situation when you were able to let things be and trust God for the outcome? What was that experience like?

What are some things in your life that you try extra hard to control, and why do you think that is?

Is there one particular thing you'd like to loosen your grip on, and what simple step can you take toward doing that?

Respond

When it comes to sustaining a sense of hope on our journey, patience plays a big role. Think about it: Every time we start grasping for control of those things that only God can work out in our lives, we start to feed our doubt that He is able and willing to take care of us. One of the most helpful things we can do for ourselves is to intentionally practice patience in the little things, so that when we're facing the not-so-little ones, we've developed more spiritual strength to handle them. This begins by simply noticing when we feel anxious or frustrated by something we can't control—long lines at the store, stubborn stoplights, maybe a person who's talking our ear off when we *really just want to get home!* It's so familiar for most of us to feel impatient in those situations that we forget there is another way to be. Challenge yourself to become more aware of those times when you feel anxious about a delay. Practice taking a deep breath, come back to the moment, and shift your thoughts toward gratitude: *Thank You, Lord, for your perfect timing*. Remember that while you may feel "stuck" somewhere, God has allowed you to be in that very spot for reasons you may not understand. As that simple shift toward gratitude becomes a habit, you'll notice yourself relaxing and breathing more easily in everyday situations that used to stress you out. And, most importantly, when you face those more significant situations that could cause doubt and discouragement to take over, you may surprise yourself with the patience muscles you've developed. God's timing is God's timing, in the big and little things, and the more we lean into that, the greater our sense of hope and contentment can be.

Hope is being able to see that there is light despite all the darkness.

DESMOND TUTU

Growing Brighter

One thing we all share as God's creations is the need for light—both the sunshiny kind and the spiritual kind! We're just drawn to it, whether it be the morning sun beaming through the kitchen window or the warm love of Jesus shining through the heart of a friend. If we find ourselves spending too much time in the dark—of any kind—we can really start to feel it. Our hearts weren't created to live in the shadows; they were made to thrive in the radiance of God's goodness and truth. There's a popular science fair project that illustrates this wonderfully, and it's something we can remember during the ups and downs of our spiritual journeys. Here's how it goes: A seed is planted in a small container, which is set in the bottom of a big box. The box has been turned into a maze, filled with obstacles, with the seed at the very bottom and a hole cut all the way up at the top, where light is coming through. Over time, as the plant grows, it naturally finds its way around the barriers of the maze and up toward the hole. Why? Because it was designed to reach toward the light, and no matter what gets in its way in the darkness, that plant will not be deterred. It's not about how big those barriers are or how many twists and turns that vine has to take, it's simply about being irresistibly drawn toward the brightness above. And isn't that how our journey happens too?

Can you recall a time in your life that felt "dim" and discouraging, and what do you think was happening to cause it?

Is there any area of your life today where God might be nudging you to grow more toward the light? Write about it here.

If you imagine yourself like that vine in the experiment, what obstacles would you say you struggle with most on your journey?

What are some ways you've had the opportunity to be a light for others?

Who in your life seems to shine brightly with the light of Christ, and how have they made a difference for you?

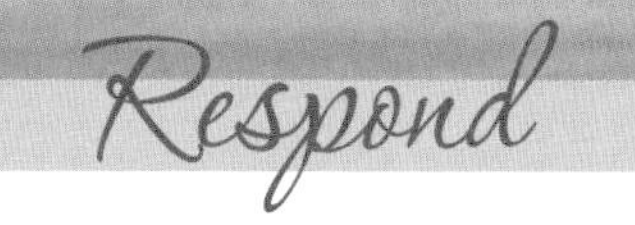

We each grow through the maze of this life differently, but the most important thing for all of us is not the challenges we have to overcome, but the fact that we have a very present, loving Creator who's always there, willing to illuminate our path if we are paying attention.

Consider the verses below—just a few of the many messages about light in God's Word. Does any message in particular speak to your heart today about your own journey?

- Your eye is the lamp of your body. When your eyes are healthy, your whole body also is full of light. But when they are unhealthy, your body also is full of darkness. —Luke 11:34 NIV
- You are all children of the light and children of the day. We do not belong to the night or to the darkness. —I Thessalonians 5:5 NIV
- Your word is a lamp for my feet, a light on my path. —Psalm 119:105 NIV
- The LORD is my light and my salvation—whom shall I fear? The LORD is the stronghold of my life—of whom shall I be afraid? —Psalm 27:1 NIV
- The city does not need the sun or the moon to shine on it, for the glory of God gives it light, and the Lamb is its lamp. —Revelation 21:23 NIV

Consider writing a note for your future self to read when things feel discouraging. How would you remind yourself to look for the light in tough times? We all need that nudge once in a while, and who better to give your heart a pep talk than the person who knows you best? You!

Almost everything will work again if you unplug it for a few minutes, including you.

ANNE LAMOTT

Finding Balance

Most of us have experienced that feeling of bone-deep exhaustion at some point in our lives. We may each arrive at the end of our ropes in different ways, but when we get there, we all know how it feels. We may wonder how we're ever going to pull ourselves back up again, and how the world is possibly going to go on without us in the meantime. We have people to show up for, after all! And stuff to make, and things to attend! But just the thought of putting more effort toward anything feels quite overwhelming at the moment. The longer we live in that tension between "*I can't do this anymore*" and "*I gotta keep going somehow*," the more depleted we become. And, lest we forget, we can't pour from an empty cup. We cannot be any good for anyone else without taking the time to lean into the loving arms of our Father and fill up on His rest, peace, and love for us. And even though the situation above is more extreme than we may be experiencing right now, we need to remember that we usually fall into those exhaustion traps gradually. We take baby steps toward them by shaving off some sleep time here and there, ignoring that red flag our bodies have been waving, taking on one project too many when we know full well it's not in our best interest, but...we think it's such a good cause and maybe this time we'll develop some sort of superpower that pulls us through! We might imagine our Creator standing nearby in those moments, watching us make those unhealthy choices, shaking His head lovingly and waiting for us to utter the one word that'll surely come from our hearts soon: "*HELP!*"

Can you recall a time when you felt that sense of bone-deep exhaustion, and how did you get through it?

How often do you catch yourself making compromises to your well-being so that you can get ahead or feel like you've done enough? Why do you think you do this?

How much rest do you allow yourself to get at night, and if you're honest, do you think you need more?

Do you feel a sense of energy and balance in your day-to-day life, and if not, how do you think you're being depleted?

What's one small step you can take toward creating space to rest in God's arms today?

Respond

Few of us want to hear this these days, because it sounds so impractical and impossible, but... *we need to find ways to unplug, regularly*. That might mean setting aside some time for quiet walks, designating one evening a week with devices turned off, or allowing for naps or peaceful times of prayer or quiet activities that fill our hearts and bring us back to ourselves. *We must be intentional about taking care of us* because no one else knows what we need like we do. In fact, we don't even know what we need like God does! That's why asking Him for little ways to find greater peace and balance in our lives is a great place to start. Those small daily things we are led to do (or *un*-do) can add up to a very big difference in the long run. And if you happen to be experiencing one of those "end-of-your-rope" times right now, be tender with yourself. Try to care for yourself like you would someone in your life whom you dearly love. Become okay with saying "no" to others for a while so that you can say "yes" to you. Every time you make a healthy choice in your life, you recognize your God-given worth. "Don't you know that you yourselves are God's temple and that God's Spirit dwells in your midst?" I Corinthians 3:16 (NIV) reminds us. Next time you're tempted to push yourself too far or deny yourself the rest you know you need, remember that truth. The world will keep turning, and God will always give you a way to show up when you need to and find rest when you don't.

There's only one corner of the universe you can be certain of improving, and that's your own self.

ALDOUS HUXLEY

Change Your Mind

How do you feel when you hear the words: *That's just the way I am, or That's just the way it is.* It may be in the middle of an argument when one person is asking for the other to do something differently. Or during a discussion about the challenging circumstances someone is facing. There's a sense of defeat in those statements—an assumption that nothing's going to change, so why bother trying? Yes, acknowledging the reality of things is important. It gives us a starting point. But God would surely remind us, when we are facing those seemingly impossible situations, to keep our hearts open to possibility—trusting that He is working in the midst of it all in His way and in His time. Meanwhile, we can remember this: *Even if nothing appears to be changing in that difficult relationship or situation, we always have the freedom to choose how we will experience it*. That means we can wake up tomorrow with a completely different outlook than we had today, simply because we changed our minds. We can be inspired by Paul's invitation in Romans 12:2 (TLB): "Don't copy the behavior and customs of this world, but be a new and different person with a fresh newness in all you do and think. Then you will learn from your own experience how His ways will really satisfy you." It's true: we can always choose hope over despair, peace over worry, grace over grumbling, gratitude over complaint. Sure, it takes some practice, but as it becomes more natural for us, we will have the capacity for greater joy and satisfaction within us, regardless of what we're facing in our lives.

Describe a situation or relationship in your life right now that you wish could be different in some way.

What do you need to choose more of today? hope? peace? grace? gratitude? And why?

How do you counsel others in your life when they are facing something that feels discouraging or impossible?

What does it mean to you to have the "mind of Christ" (1 Corinthians 2:16)?

When you wake up tomorrow morning, how might you set your thoughts on a positive path for the day ahead?

Respond

Try this exercise to help illustrate the power of your thoughts in determining how you experience your life. Find a familiar place—maybe a room in your home, your backyard, your office... anywhere you spend a good amount of time. Now, look around that place and find every negative thing about it that you possibly can. Maybe it's dusty, there's a stain on the rug, the grass needs mowed, the neighbor's dog is noisy, that computer is outdated...you get the idea. Imagine looking through the lens of a pessimist and really pay attention to how it makes you feel. Then, close your eyes for a moment, take a deep breath, clear your mind, open your eyes, and look around again. This time, look for all the good. The sun is shining. You hear the sweet song of a bird. You're blessed to have a safe, comfortable home to live in. That drink you're sipping is warm and delicious. There is no end to the blessings you can count. In fact, you may notice that you can naturally list more good things than bad. God's gifts are infinite; we simply fail to recognize them sometimes in our day-to-day lives. So back to those tough relationships and situations. How are they being affected by your state of mind? How have you been thinking about them? How would you *like* to think about them? Remember: you *always* have the freedom to choose your experience. Prayerfully consider whether there are some adjustments you can make *within* that will help you live with more peace, joy, and contentment, regardless of whether you see a change in anything (or anyone) else right now. You can trust that God is always working in your circumstances, and even before you witness the fruit of that, you can choose to enjoy the journey.

There's never been a single moment when God was not with you.

ANONYMOUS

Your Biggest Moments

There have been times in history when much of the world seemed to pause, hold our collective breath, and acknowledge the immensity of a moment. If you lived through the '80s, for instance, you've probably had someone ask where you were on that fateful day when the space shuttle *Challenger* was launched—a mission that never reached its destination. Or maybe you, or someone you know, was blessed to witness a more joyous occasion in space: those first triumphant steps of Neil Armstrong on the moon. Something about the communal response of hundreds, thousands, or even millions of people makes an event feel very significant—and for good reason! There are defining moments and turning points in history that can affect all of us for generations to come. But there are also those more private monumental moments that we experience as individuals, which are just as earth-shattering for us, personally, even if they don't happen for all the world to see. And while our loved ones may have witnessed and shared in some of them, other things have been ours to walk through alone. And that can feel a little lonely when we realize that, try as they might, no one else on the planet can understand exactly how it feels to be in our shoes because, well...they're *our* shoes! It's tough when big things are happening for us (both the wonderful and not-so-wonderful) and nobody seems to comprehend the immensity of it all like we do. Guess who *does* understand it though...every detail? Our audience of One. The One who made us and knows us, inside and out.

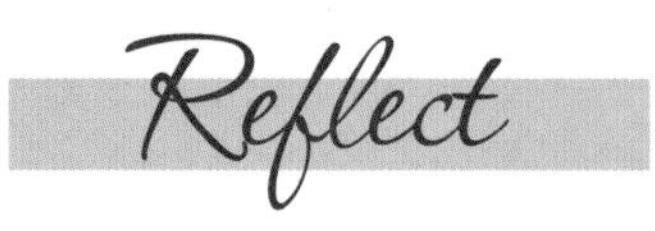

Can you think of one of those significant moments in history you've been present for, and how it felt to be part of a collective experience?

What are some of the more private monumental moments you've had in your life thus far?

Describe a time you experienced something very profound, but you felt like no one could truly understand how significant it was for you.

When you feel like you're facing something alone, how do you remind yourself of God's presence with you?

Think of a few people in the Bible who experienced things that others didn't seem to understand—how did they lean into God, trusting that He was with them through it all?

Respond

Here's a simple, healing thing you can do to remind yourself of God's presence throughout your life, especially in those times when you may have felt unnoticed, unappreciated, or just plain alone. First, take out your journal or a sketch pad—this is something you can write about or draw if you want to get creative! (Stick figures are welcome...no judgment...this is for your eyes only!) Make a list of (or sketch out) a few of the most monumental moments in your life that you can remember—both happy and difficult times—whether they were obvious to others or known only to you. Recall as many details as you can...how it happened, who was there, what you felt, how it affected your life moving forward, maybe in ways you didn't even realize at the time. Acknowledging the significance of what we've been through can be a helpful, healing thing, and sometimes it gives us some closure we didn't even realize we needed. When you are finished sharing, take a few moments to read these words of the psalmist:

You have searched me, Lord, and you know me.
You know when I sit and when I rise; you perceive my thoughts from afar.
You discern my going out and my lying down; you are familiar with all my ways.
Before a word is on my tongue you, Lord, know it completely.
You hem me in behind and before, and you lay your hand upon me.
Such knowledge is too wonderful for me, too lofty for me to attain.
—Psalm 139:1–6 NIV

Be reminded once again of God's nearness, of His deep and complete understanding of your heart, and His commitment to be there for all your moments, great and small, for all eternity.

Hope is a passion for the possible.

SØREN KIERKEGAARD

The Light of Hope

When we look back on our collective history—the history of humankind—we can surely see those times when darkness seemed to dominate. But if we could somehow zoom in very closely, we would also be able to see, against the backdrop of that darkness, points of light that shine like stars in the night sky. And those points of light would be the people who never gave up hope in the midst of our world's most difficult times. They're the ones who dared to dream of brighter days when others had decided that things would never get better. The ones who kept trying, kept taking small steps toward positive change, even if no one believed it made any difference...even if their efforts went unnoticed and unappreciated. And though most of those shining souls never made it into headlines or history books, they're the ones who kept the candle burning for the rest of us, and that's a much bigger deal than we may realize. Who knows what kind of world we'd live in today if they had not each done their small but mighty part? It seems that our beautiful Creator placed a treasure within each of us when He made us, and that was the capacity for hope. To believe in what we can't yet see, and to trust that, as Jesus reminds us in Matthew 19:26 (NLT), "Humanly speaking, it is impossible. But with God everything is possible." When we place our hope in Christ, it can spark wildfires of goodness. And that's just what happened for many of those people throughout history who knew and walked with Him.

How would you describe the time we're living in?

What would you like to see happening more in the world around you, and is there any small step you could take to be part of that change?

Who do you see holding a candle of hope for others?

What opportunities have you been given to do your "small but mighty" part in your little corner of the world?

How would you describe the difference between just "hoping for the best" and placing that hope in Christ?

God is calling people everywhere, every day to shine His light of hope for the world. And often, that happens in simple, subtle ways that make a bigger difference than we realize. Here are two things we can do when we find ourselves feeling discouraged about the state of our community or our culture or even our great big world.

1. We can become more intentionally aware of the people who are doing all they can to share the hope of Christ around us. Maybe we can give them a pat on the back they aren't expecting, just to let them know they *are* making a difference, even if it doesn't feel like it sometimes. We can be inspired by their courage and compassion as we witness the ways they follow God's leading to serve those He brings into their lives.

2. We can ask in prayer how we, too, might be a light for others. And even if we don't sense a specific response right away, we can trust that in His time, God will reveal those answers to us. We need to remember that often, He may nudge us toward some very practical, down-to-earth actions we can take. And those can be quite spontaneous: He might simply whisper to our hearts in the moment: "*That waitress could really use a word of encouragement today*" or "*See that teacher? He's overwhelmed, and he needs to know he's making a difference*" or "*Don't be afraid to share that new idea you have with the other volunteers; it's a good one!*" Regardless of when, or how, He calls us, we always have the choice about whether to answer that call. He loves us no matter what we choose, but He knows the joy it can bring to our hearts when we step into those opportunities to light the world with His love.

Deep within us all there is an amazing inner sanctuary... a holy place.

THOMAS RAYMOND KELLY

Here's a wonderful thing about you that you may need reminded of from time to time: There is a part of you, deep within, that is absolutely *untouchable*. No one in all creation gets access to that part of you: No one except your Maker. We're talking about the "you" behind your thoughts, beyond your beliefs and your expectations and your actions. We're talking about the unique and beautiful soul you are that God breathed into existence and called "good." The one looking out through your eyes, laughing your laugh, and learning to live as a spiritual being in a physical world. Yes, God gave you a body that allows you to experience His creation in countless ways. He gave you a mind to make sense of things, to create and imagine and believe. But beneath all of that is the heart of you, made in His image, enlivened by His Spirit, loved and protected from every force that would seek to dim your light. Does this mean you feel the truth of that all the time? No, of course not. Does it destroy every doubt and fear you face as you navigate your everyday life? Nope. But the more often you pause to remember who (and whose) you are, the more courage, hope, and untouchable joy you can experience in life. Because we know those things don't come from the outside, as much as the world would try to convince us otherwise. They come from deep within.

Think of a few things (or people) that seem to get you down repeatedly. Why do you think that is?

What would it feel like if you didn't let these situations or relationships affect you negatively? How would your life change?

Do you sometimes catch yourself being carried away by your thoughts, and how do you re-center yourself?

Do you know anyone who seems "unruffled" by the things that often bother others, and what do you observe about their life?

How do you envision that sacred, untouchable part of you where you connect deeply with God?

Here's an exercise that can help remind you of that peaceful place at your center, where you can experience God's presence deeply, beyond all the noise. Even practicing it a few times a week can help you start to move through your daily life with an unwavering hope. Find a quiet spot and a comfortable position and set a timer for ten minutes with the sole intention to just *be*. That may seem like a short amount of time, but when your goal is to do absolutely nothing but show up and breathe, it can feel like an eternity! Sitting quietly makes us very aware of how noisy our minds can be. But it also reminds us of this powerful truth: *We are much more than our thoughts*. That chatter in our heads is not who we are, and it can't control or affect us in any way unless we allow it. The more we learn to simply observe our train of thought in those times of quiet, the more naturally it will come and go. Then, when we find ourselves out in the world, encountering the circumstances and relationships that usually hijack our minds and cause us to feel upset or discouraged, we can experience them with more peace and acceptance. We can take a deep breath, let those thoughts go, and return to that awareness of God's Spirit within us, receiving the promise found in Isaiah: "You will keep in perfect peace all who trust in You, all whose thoughts are fixed on You!" (Isaiah 26:3 NLT). Remember: you have the God-given ability to shift out of doubt and frustration anytime, anywhere, and back into the peace He provides in that sacred place within.

Outside our comfort zone is where we experience the true awesomeness of God.

LYSA TERKEURST

The Gift of Discomfort

Okay, take a deep breath before reading this because it's a tough pill to swallow: *Discomfort is a very important experience in our lives.* "What?!?" we might exclaim, recalling that awful rainy campout that ended our outdoorsy career, those too-tight pants we can't seem to let go of, or even the awkwardness of running into someone at the grocery store who makes us feel, well...*uncomfortable*. There's something about discomfort that wakes us up, forces us to shift out of autopilot and into our bodies, and frankly, just reminds us how very human we are. Wouldn't you know that God, in His infinite wisdom, happens to have the perfect recipe for using discomfort for our growth. Whether it be facing an illness, the intimidating learning curve of a new job, lack of sleep due to that infant who's suddenly taken over our house—most of us are facing at least something in our lives that we wish was easier. And while our Creator doesn't "send" things to hurt us, He absolutely uses *everything* to help us. Whatever discomfort you are experiencing in your life today—whether it feels heavily burdensome or just mildly annoying—He is always inviting you to "grow through what you go through." Whether you decide to accept that invitation is, of course, up to you.

Describe a time you experienced discomfort that ended up bringing about a blessing in your life.

Describe a time you took the "easy way out" of something, only to realize that you missed an opportunity that was hidden within it.

Is there anything you enjoy today that you used to avoid because you feared it would be uncomfortable? Write about your experience.

Write about how you deal with the most uncomfortable things in life. Do you look for the lesson in them, find ways to avoid them at all costs, or maybe try to numb the experience as much as you can?

Who do you know that seems to step outside their comfort zone more often than most, and how do they inspire you?

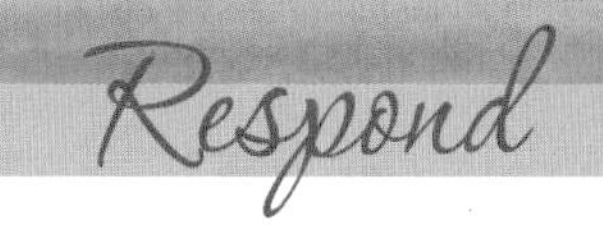

Here's a challenge that can help increase your self-awareness about your own "comfort zones" and inspire you to expand your life experience. Hope you're ready! Find one thing to do that makes you more than a little uncomfortable this week. We're not talking about taking a bite of that one vegetable you despise or setting the thermostat a few degrees in the wrong direction. Find something that will take some courage and determination on your part. It could be making a phone call to someone you've felt distant from lately, choosing to fast for part of a day, or trying a new activity you've felt very intimidated by. The important thing is that your experience causes you to become more aware of your thoughts and feelings in those moments. Ask yourself things like: *Why have I avoided this? What am I resisting, and can I allow myself to stay present long enough to feel it?* And most importantly, *How might God use this discomfort to help me grow?* We don't realize it in the moment, of course, but once we get a little distance from a situation, we might see that it expanded us in some new way. Whether that be gaining a deeper sense of courage within ourselves or greater compassion for what others go through in life. We might become more aware of the feelings we try to avoid in our lives, and that's important, because avoiding feelings makes our world smaller; we dodge certain people and situations trying to protect ourselves, and in doing so, we may miss out on opportunities. Bottom line: *Discomfort is only a bad thing if we choose to experience it that way.* Allow God to work in it, and you may be pleasantly surprised at what He has to show you in the process.

God's purpose
shines through everything;
it's up to us to discover it.

ANONYMOUS

Sacred Seeing

When you go outside and look up on a clear night, do you see pictures and patterns among the stars, or do you see random, brilliant points of light scattered across the dark sky? The answer to that question likely depends on what you've learned throughout your life. At some point, you may have been taught about constellations. Many of us grew up hearing stories that have been passed down for generations, inviting us to connect the dots and imagine things like those five stars there on the horizon, forming an animal or a cross or a bow and arrow. Once someone points out a pattern or connection that we're able to see clearly, it's often hard to un-see. We can walk outside and tell ourselves we're just looking at a bunch of unrelated dots, but those stories have made pictures in our minds, and these minds of ours are quite impressionable! This is a wonderful thing to remember when we're struggling with a sense of purpose or meaning in our lives. God's Word is like our constellation map; it's our forever reminder that we live in a much larger story; that nothing is random; that every little thing matters, and not only that, but it's all part of a beautiful picture that's slowly coming into view over time. When we find ourselves doubting that truth, we can often trace it back to our connection with Him. We need to draw close and be reminded, once again, that the dots in our lives are connected by His design, even when we don't always understand how.

What is happening in your life right now that you'd like to have a clearer understanding of?

Describe a time when you struggled to make sense of something you experienced, and later discovered some meaning in it.

What is the most challenging area of your life when it comes to trusting that God has a purpose?

Name someone you know who seems to experience life as a random series of events—what do you observe about them?

Name someone you know who looks for purpose in everything—what do you observe about them?

Respond

So how can we remind ourselves that every detail matters in God's design? Proverbs 3:5–6 describes three things we can do regularly in our lives:

1. Trust in the Lord with all your heart.

That's a lot of trust He's asking for! But we know He is more than worthy of it. And it doesn't happen for us all at once, of course. Trust grows moment by moment, both through our everyday experiences and in the middle of those more epic events we encounter. We learn to turn our hearts toward Him often and whisper, "*I know that you're working in this.*"

2. Do not lean on your own understanding.

It isn't easy to give our own understanding a back seat, but there's a deeper sense of knowing that comes only from our Maker. When we're feeling lost or discouraged, we can always choose to lean into Him for greater vision and clarity.

3. In all your ways acknowledge Him.

To "acknowledge" means "to admit the existence or truth of." Our life experiences can be so much more meaningful and satisfying when we acknowledge God's presence in the midst of them. This can be as quiet as a prayer whispered in our hearts or as exuberant as the praise we shout from the rooftops. He delights in our acknowledgment, just as we delight in His.

This passage ends with the promise that, "He will make your paths straight." While each of our paths will look different, we can trust that every step we take has purpose, and He knows exactly where He's leading us. There's a lot of peace to be found in that truth.

*Live your life
for an audience of One.*

ANONYMOUS

Reputation can be a tricky thing. If you've ever been the subject of hurtful gossip or someone has intentionally tried to convince others of something negative about you, then you know exactly what that means. Many of us were raised in families who valued having a "good name," and for good reason! Whether it be in friendships, jobs, ministry positions or other relationships, people can be reluctant to build connections with someone who is generally considered untrustworthy or unreliable. And we, as followers of Jesus, called to speak truth, model integrity, and love well—we do what we can to live with good character. *But*... that doesn't always guarantee that we will keep ourselves out of the rumor mill. Sometimes, it's just out of our hands. As hard as it is to admit, there are people in the world—and sometimes in our own lives—who are determined, for whatever reason, to drag us down. It may be their own insecurities, envy, misdirected anger—only God knows, and it's really not our job to figure it out. But what we *can* control is our own thoughts, our intentions, and our actions. The more we keep our focus on those things and off other people's interpretations and opinions about our lives...the better off we will be.

Were you encouraged to keep up a good image by your caregivers growing up, and did you ever struggle with that?

Have you ever been the subject of hurtful gossip, and if so, how did it make you feel?

What do you do when you hear someone start to speak negatively about another?

What do you do when you're aware that someone has made a judgment or is speaking negatively about you?

Read the words of Proverbs 15:4 (NLT): "Gentle words are a tree of life; a deceitful tongue crushes the spirit." How have you seen that play out in your life?

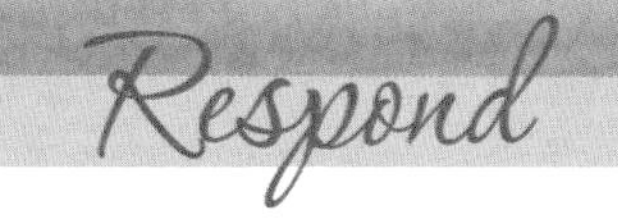

Even if you aren't dealing right now with someone else's judgment or misunderstanding about you, there are people everywhere who are being hurt by others' negative opinions and accusations. One way we can all be a light in this area is to model integrity. Our integrity doesn't hinge on anyone else's ideas about us; it is our desire to live right from the inside out, because that's what God calls us to do. We were created for that kind of authenticity, and when we're not living it, it will take its toll, eventually. Not only does integrity help protect us from the sting of others' criticism by giving us a more solid sense of ourselves, but it also keeps us from trying to put up a false front to impress them. There's no need for a facade when we have nothing to hide. Choosing to live with integrity is the difference between projecting a movie about ourselves for the world to see, and actually living out the truth of our lives without apology, no matter who's in the audience or what kind of review we may get. Pay attention in the coming days to how you feel from the inside out. Are your decisions and actions coming from your heart, or are they heavily influenced by the way others might perceive you? And what happens when you hear someone speaking negatively about another person? Even if it's someone you don't know or a celebrity, they are just as human and worthy of love as we are, no matter what stories we've heard or opinions we've formed. Let's be the light for others to live kindly and authentically. And be encouraged if you're the one feeling mistreated or misunderstood. Your loving Father knows the whole truth of you, and gently reminds you that your heart will always be what matters most to Him.

Every happening, great and small, is a parable whereby God speaks to us, and the art of life is to get the message.

MALCOLM MUGGERIDGE

Expect the Unexpected

We don't have to spend much time in the New Testament to notice that Jesus often spoke in parables. They're stories anyone can relate to, regardless of status or human intelligence; they challenge people to think in new ways about timeless truths; and, perhaps most importantly, parables just have a way of entering our hearts first...before our brains have time to fit them into a structure or system that we're already comfortable with. In short: *Jesus had a back-door way of reaching people*. That's how He was able to enter a culture where many folks had become bound by religious rules and blinded by self-righteousness, and He blew it up lovingly, from the inside out. And like those people He lived among, we sometimes find ourselves spending more time in our heads than our hearts too. We can tell when that starts to happen, in fact, because we start feeling a little empty, spiritually. We miss that wonderful sense of God's presence, and so we start looking around for it—usually through the "front door" of our lives, in all those expected ways we've come to know Him. But we may soon discover that He's been knocking on the *back doors* of our hearts all along. Just like Jesus did through the telling of those parables, God is always inviting us into new ways of experiencing Him, and often He will use those times when we've felt spiritually "meh" to be catalysts for our growth.

What's one of Jesus' parables that particularly speaks to you?

Can you name a movie or book of fiction that inspired you in some unexpected way by taking that back-door route to your heart?

Describe a time when you couldn't sense God's presence in your life, even though you knew He was there.

How do you deal with those seasons when you feel a little "dry" spiritually? Name some ways you try to sense God's presence again in your life.

Write about a time when you experienced God in a new or unexpected way.

Respond

Because we are all created uniquely, our Maker knows we each have different ways of experiencing His presence. He also knows that to grow in our understanding and awareness of Him in our daily lives, we must be nudged out of our comfort zones. Sometimes that means letting one well run dry, so we'll seek out another. Think of Jesus telling those parables to a riveted audience. They most likely expected things to go a certain way in His stories, but at some point, they were challenged with the unexpected, made to go deeper into their hearts to discover what their heads couldn't make sense of. Today, He's doing the same for us. We're constantly being invited to grow in Him and become aware of Him in new ways. Sometimes that feels quite uncomfortable. If you're facing a time of not feeling God's nearness, here are a few simple steps you can take:

1. *Remember the truth.* No matter what your experience is at the moment, He is as near to you as He has ever been, and He will never, ever leave you.

2. *Ask for help.* Ask Him to help you understand what's making you feel distant or "meh" about your connection. Is there something you need to look at? Are you paying attention?

3. *Open your heart.* Be intentional about looking for Him in your daily life and know that He surely delights in that. Jeremiah 29:13 (NLT) reminds us: "If you look for me wholeheartedly, you will find me." Your heart was designed to seek Him, and if you are open to it, He will show up in ways you never imagined. You may look back one day and see that those times of feeling "emptier" actually prepared you to be filled even more with His love.

One day you will look back and see that all along you were blooming.

MORGAN HARPER NICHOLS

Living Well

It's not surprising to learn that people who live the longest tend to share a list of common traits. And while some of those traits can vary, most can be traced right back to biblical truth. We're talking about more than just clean livin', although that's certainly a factor when it comes to helping our bodies thrive into our later years. But studies also reveal that a positive, hopeful outlook on life is one of the main determiners of longevity. And that's not a new realization. Nearly three thousand years ago, King Solomon declared: "A cheerful heart is good medicine, but a crushed spirit dries up the bones" (Proverbs 17:22 NIV). He was definitely onto something! But what we can sometimes forget is that a cheerful heart takes intention. Most people who are known as "glass-half-full" folks didn't get there by accident. They chose it, and they keep choosing it every day. Sure, genetics may affect our disposition to some degree, but there's something even more powerful determining how we see the world: *The power of our own free will*. We always have the freedom to choose what we'll focus on in our lives. And it's not a one-and-done decision. It's a daily turning of our hearts toward all that's good and true, no matter what that day brings. And we all know that some days offer plenty of reasons to feel discouraged. Those are the days that matter most when it comes to our spiritual growth. Because it's easy to be cheerful when the sun is out, but when the storms come? That's when we find out what we're really made of. Those positive people we admire, who have learned to look for silver linings—it's quite likely they've had to experience some pretty tough times in order to find out what it takes to rise above it all.

Is there an older person in your life whom you look up to as an example of aging positively? Why do you look up to him or her?

Envision yourself a decade or two older than you are now; what are your greatest hopes for that person?

In what ways are you intentional about turning your heart toward the goodness in each day?

Who inspires you with their genuinely hopeful heart—regardless of their circumstances—and what might you learn from them?

What's one thing you can do when you wake up tomorrow morning to remind yourself to choose joy?

Respond

Novelist Annie Dillard once observed, "How we spend our days is of course how we spend our lives." As we look back and reflect on life from our later years, we will surely discover how true that statement is. A beautiful life doesn't happen by accident; we choose it one thought at a time, one action at a time, one day at a time. And that takes some real intention, especially in the more difficult seasons we go through. We must remember that no matter what we're facing, we are always free to shift our focus toward "what is true, and honorable, and right, and pure, and lovely, and admirable" (Philippians 4:8 NLT). And in doing so, we allow our most difficult times to bring forth unexpected goodness. In fact, James 1:2 (NLT) calls us beyond just tolerating our troubles; it challenges us to "consider it an opportunity for great joy" when we face the tough stuff. Which sounds lovely in theory, but how do we walk that out in real life? Well, first of all, we start today. Even if it means starting small...even if there's nothing big and ugly staring us in the face at the moment. Each time we redirect a thought from fear to faith, each time we choose a word of affirmation over a complaint, each time we lift someone up instead of discouraging them—we're adding a brick to that beautiful life we're building. As we heed the wisdom of Ephesians 4:23 (CEV)—"Let the Spirit change your way of thinking"—those good thoughts will grow into actions...that's just how it works! And so one day, we will be able to look back and see a life well-lived.

Never be afraid
to trust an unknown future
to a known God.

CORRIE TEN BOOM

Behind the Scenes

Have you ever been sitting near a window with sunlight streaming through, and you suddenly notice tiny flecks floating in the air? It may look like dust or bits of fuzz, but whatever it is, you didn't notice it until the sun's angle was just right and it revealed the presence of something you had no idea was drifting about. Then, you start to realize that those itty-bitty particles are floating around everywhere in your house; you just don't usually see them. How do you know they're everywhere? Take a look at your air conditioner filter sometime. That stuff's gotta come from somewhere! Here's the point: Just because we can't see something all the time doesn't mean it's not there affecting us somehow. We get so used to focusing on those obvious things right in front of us, we sometimes forget what can be going on behind the scenes. Our spiritual lives are no different...and that is a helpful, hopeful thing to remember, especially when we're walking through something tough that feels like it's taking forever. We might be seeking God's guidance in a particular situation and wondering if we'll ever find our way. We could be praying for relief from an ongoing struggle. And if we're honest, many of us have reached a point before when we threw up our hands and cried, "*Is anyone really listening at all???*" Of course, we know the answer to that; we know that God is good, and real, and so very present—even on days when we just can't feel it. But sometimes we do need a reminder that it's all going to be okay in the end, even if we don't quite understand how.

Is there anything you feel very uncertain about in your life right now, and how are you handling it?

Write about your patience level…do you often find yourself frustrated with unanswered prayers, or are you able to trust more in God's timing?

Can you recall a time when you felt confused about what was happening in your life, and God worked it out in an unexpected way? Write about it.

What advice would you give someone who's facing a painful, frustrating, or confusing situation, and can you receive that wisdom into your own heart?

Can you think of a biblical story that illustrates the truth that God is always working behind the scenes in ways we may not realize? Write it here.

It can be tough to understand why God keeps some things hidden from our view as long as He does. We assume that if something can be found or fixed, revealed or redeemed...then *why not do it now?* We forget how limited our human perspective can be, and that's why He asks us to trust His heart and His timing. As Romans 8:28 reminds us, He's always working for the highest good of those who love Him. And that includes *you*. So what can you do during those times of waiting and wondering how things are going to work out? Let's return for a moment to those dust particles floating around. Remember: They're always there, but we only glimpse them when they're revealed by the sunlight. We will never see *all* of them at the same time, but we can see a *few* of them when conditions are right. The same is true for us spiritually. When you're feeling discouraged about a situation or season in your life, take a moment to ask your heavenly Father for some glimmers of hope. Be as honest as you can about your frustrations and fears; allow your heart to speak freely, and just lay it all out there. He can take it! Ask Him to help you believe in what you can't see right now. Remember: Just because you're dealing with doubt doesn't mean you don't trust Him. It just means you need to feel His nearness most in times of uncertainty, like a child who reaches for her father's hand. Ask Him for that reassurance and be open to all the ways He might provide it. Even if the bigger things are still being worked out behind the scenes, the silver linings He offers are always available to those of us with eyes to see.

Art is a reflection of God's creativity, an evidence that we are made in the image of God.

FRANCIS SCHAEFFER

From Head to Heart

Whether or not you would describe yourself as a "creative" person, it's likely that some form of art has inspired you at some point in your life. It could be anything from live theater to paintings to gardening to exquisite culinary presentations. Creativity is everywhere, and unless we are determined to resist it, something will usually find its way in to touch us somehow. Why might this be important in the big picture of our lives? Because it helps to give us greater balance between our heads and our hearts—especially those among us who tend to overthink or often feel a bit "trapped" in our minds. We get a kind of tunnel vision, and things start to look very dark and serious. We see less beauty and possibility and experience more worry and fear, and it can be tough to free ourselves from that cycle once it begins. Those are the moments when we most need to take that eighteen-inch (or so) journey from our heads to our hearts. We need a greater sense of hope and lightness and freedom. And a wonderful way to get us there is creativity. This could be as simple as listening to an uplifting song, making something with our hands, or looking at a book of beautiful photography. God seems to have designed us in such a way that art—in whatever form we're drawn to—is able to bring us back to the moment, refresh us, and offer us a respite from whatever is weighing us down.

What are your favorite kinds of art, and how do you find ways to experience them?

Do you like to create, or witness others' creativity—or both? Explain why or why not.

Do you ever struggle with a "hamster wheel" of thoughts in your mind, and if so, what do you do to find peace?

What's one activity that makes you feel childlike?

Are there any creative endeavors you've always wanted to try, and what has stopped you?

Most of us have heard of or read Jesus' well-known invitation for His followers to "become like little children." There's a lot to unpack about what He's saying, but for our purposes here, let's consider that children are generally more open-minded, less self-conscious, and able to be present in the moment, unlike many adults who are constantly evaluating, planning, dreading... you get the picture. This is why the youngest (and most young-hearted) among us are so much freer to create. It's also why those of us who struggle most with worry and overthinking could benefit greatly from allowing art—in whatever form uniquely speaks to us—to offer us a recess from our "big, important" thoughts. It can be both refreshing and healing for us to take that intentional trip from our heads to our hearts and surrender to the moment, and we do it far less than we could. So here's your challenge, should you choose to accept it: Find one form of art to enjoy in the week ahead. Set aside even a half hour (set a timer if helps you to let go a little easier) and let it be a time of pure enjoyment. Whether you're observing someone else's creations or experiencing your own, just be aware of God's presence with you in the moment and know that He delights in your childlike spirit. We need to remember this especially when we're going through tough times; art can help to heal and bring hope to our hearts in ways we may not realize. We're made in the image of the ultimate Creator, after all. Surely, His plans for us include some unique and beautiful creations of our own.

If you change nothing,
nothing changes.

JOYCE BROTHERS

Spinning Our Wheels

Have you ever heard yourself say something like, "*I just feel so stuck right now.*" That feeling visits all of us, in one way or another, at different times in our lives. Whether it's a goal we're aiming for, a relationship we're working on, or just life in general. We sometimes reach a point when we just don't sense any forward movement or positive change; we can't see the path ahead clearly, and we're simply tired of standing still. Now this experience of "stuckness" would be a real bummer if we were limited to the world's resources to get us moving again. You know, all those things that promise us success and happiness if we just read that book, listen to that speaker, or follow that social media account? Of course, it's true that there are some great tools out there to help us on our way, but it can be a little overwhelming as we try to sort through them. Who do we trust? Where do we start? Which step do we take first? Thankfully, as the psalmist reminds us in Psalm 121, we don't have to scramble for solutions. Our help comes from an infinite, loving Creator who has all we need to thrive: "I lift up my eyes to the mountains—where does my help come from? My help comes from the LORD, the Maker of heaven and earth" (Psalm 121:1–2 NIV). When our frustrated hearts are calling for our attention, we don't have to head down that rabbit hole of worry, wondering how we're going to get things moving in a hopeful direction again. We simply need to stop and ask for help.

In what area of your life do you feel a sense of "stuckness" right now?

Can you recall a time when you felt frustrated about your lack of forward movement with something, and how did you get going again?

What are your go-to resources for encouragement and guidance when you're facing something challenging in your life?

Describe the last time you faced a situation that felt impossible, but God pulled you through in an unexpected way.

Do you know anyone who seems to be stuck in their own frustrating pattern, and how might you pray for them or offer support?

If you've ever driven a car into deep snow, mud, or sand and found yourself spinning your wheels, you eventually realize that—as the well-known saying points out—it's pointless to do the same thing over and over again and expect different results. The longer you spin those wheels, the deeper the rut you create, and at some point, you have to realize that if you don't consider other options, you might as well just give up hope of ever getting anywhere. And the same goes with those frustrating situations in our lives. Sometimes it takes a while to realize that what we're doing isn't working. That's hard to admit, especially when we've poured a lot of time and effort into it. But the greatest gift we can give ourselves in those times is to stop and say a simple prayer for help. The moment we invite God to meet us in that rut is the first step toward our freedom from it. So how about your life right now? Is there any way you feel like you're spinning your wheels? Any situations or relationships that just feel stuck? If so, take a few moments to write those things down and ask God for one small step you could take toward change. You may not know how that help will come, but you can be sure that it *will* come, in His way and in His time. It may be a nudge to switch up your daily routine in some way, inspiration to pick up the phone and make a call, or maybe even to seek out the wisdom of someone who's been there. Your job is simply to listen with your heart and trust His guidance. Even if nothing changes today, you can live with that wonderful sense of hope that He's always working. And one day you will look back and see how He brought you out of that place one prayer and one step at a time.

Positive thinking must be followed by positive doing.

JOHN MAXWELL

Helping Hearts

There's a lot going on in this world of ours. Of course, we know that has always been true—we just haven't always had 24-hour news cycles. A few hundred years ago, people couldn't see what was happening on the other side of the globe; they were likely more concerned with what was going on right in front of them. And while we have the gift of being more broadly connected today, unfortunately, we also have the burden of information overload, and that can include a lot of negativity. We may find ourselves weeding through discouraging headlines, observing hurtful online exchanges between those with different convictions, and maybe even just wishing things didn't feel so heavy. It can be a tough environment to stay positive in, but God always makes a way, if we're paying attention. He gives us each unique opportunities to find glimmers of hope and share them with others, right where we are. In fact, whenever we pray for the "world" we can remember that we're part of it—and we're part of the answer to that prayer too. Every little step we take to bring hope makes a difference. Every time we choose gratitude over complaint, joy over discouragement, belief over despair—it matters, infinitely. Not because the whole world is suddenly changed by our small daily actions, but because God is able to take those mustard seeds of effort and grow them into beautiful things, as only He can do.

How have you felt both encouraged and discouraged about the world around you recently?

Is there anyone in your life who's known for looking on the bright side? How about someone who's more of a glass-half-empty person? Describe the difference in how you feel around them.

What's one heartwarming thing you've witnessed recently involving an act of kindness that inspired you?

What's one small thing you could do to shine a little light into your everyday world today?

Write out a verse that brings news into your home to remind you of the hope we have in Christ.

Respond

When Fred Rogers (the man known for creating the heartwarming children's television show *Mr. Rogers' Neighborhood*) was a boy, and he would see scary things in the news, his mother would tell him, "Look for the helpers. You will always find people who are helping." She was teaching him how to shift his focus away from fear and toward hope...and it's a lesson we can surely all benefit from. Give it a try in the next few days. When headlines loom or negative chatter persists, challenge yourself to rise above it and look for the hopeful things that are happening around you. They can be very simple: A barista brightening days with a warm smile, a story about a compassionate pet rescue, a neighbor giving a hand to change a tire. Those things surround us every day, and while they may not be epic events altering big global situations, they *are* simple acts of kindness, helping the hearts of people, one by one, to heal and to hope again. And as you observe those day brighteners, ask God to help you be one of them. The more often you take those opportunities to lift up your fellow humans, the more you'll be reminded that you aren't alone in doing so. There are others being called to shine His light alongside you. No matter what the news says or what the day brings, the helpers will always be there, and you can be one of them.

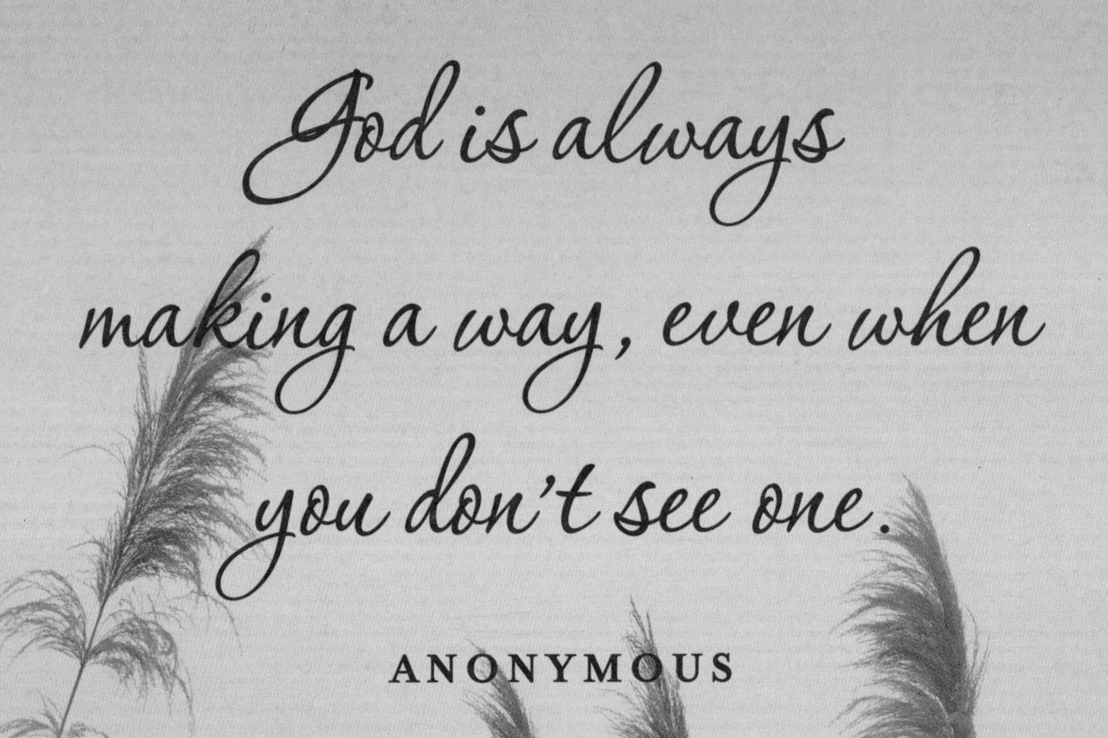

God is always making a way, even when you don't see one.

ANONYMOUS

Stop, Surrender, Be Still

You've probably heard this well-known bit of the book of Exodus, often shared to encourage those who are facing battles in their lives: "The LORD will fight for you; you need only to be still" (Exodus 14:14 NIV). While it speaks to each of us differently, depending on what we're walking through at the moment, we can all be encouraged to trust that God is absolutely able and willing to handle anything. Especially those things that feel impossible or overwhelming to us. Of course, God's *not* saying, "*Hey, start a fight and I'll finish it for you.*" But He *is* saying, in essence: "*That hard thing you're facing? I'm in it with you, all the way. Just let me take the lead.*" That message is given as He leads the Israelites through a life of slavery and into freedom. And in the same way, He speaks to people throughout history (and that includes us) who are walking though the most discouraging, disappointing, or even downright fearful times of our lives. Our battles happen for many reasons; we may have even had a hand in starting them, or we may have been blindsided by circumstances beyond our control. Regardless, the thing that matters most is that we recognize our need to surrender it all to our Maker. And as we do so, we must remember that when He fights for us, the victory may happen very differently than we envision, but it will always happen for the highest good of all who trust in Him.

What are you facing in your life right now that feels like a battle?

Have you ever gone through something that felt like more than just a human struggle—something beyond your understanding? Describe it here.

How have you seen God work in some of your (and maybe others') most difficult times?

What are some biblical stories that remind you that God will always show up, maybe even when and where you least expect it?

Who in your life inspires you with the peace they've found within, despite their difficult or uncertain circumstances? What about them inspires you?

Whether or not you're going through something big right now, there's a simple thing you can do to remind yourself of God's presence and guidance in any battles you'll face in life. Find a place to display these three words where you can see them often: *Stop. Surrender. Be still.*

1. Stop. The moment you realize you're facing something that's bigger than you, out of your hands, or seemingly impossible to make it through, it's time to stop and remember you're not meant to face it alone.

2. Surrender. This is often the hardest part, because we humans have a real knack for trying to control things in our lives. (Have you noticed?) Here is where we acknowledge that there's only One who truly understands this battle of ours, and He will provide all we need to get through it.

3. Be still. Being still doesn't mean we stop trying or pretend it's all good. It *does* mean that we turn our hearts toward God again and again in the middle of our struggles, like sunflowers toward the sun, and soak in His presence. We allow Him to reassure and guide us every step of the way. And when our minds kick into high gear wondering how in the world it's all going to work out...we breathe deeply and say, "God's got this," and we mean it. The more we surrender, the more we make room for peace.

Know what happened shortly after those words about fighting battles were delivered in Exodus 14:14? The parting of the Red Sea—that unforgettable move of God that has been shared throughout history as something absolutely impossible made possible by a divine hand. That's our God, and He still shows up in unimaginable ways to bring us victory over all we face.

May the God of hope fill you with all joy and peace as you trust in Him.

ROMANS 15:13 NIV

All We'll Ever Need

The Bible calls Jesus Christ our hope in many ways. Not only Jesus the human, who entered the mess of the world a few thousand years ago and showed people a new, more compassionate, more authentic way to live. Not only Jesus the Christ, who did what no one else could ever do for us, so that we could live in the presence of our loving Father one day—for all eternity. But the Jesus of the *now*, of our everyday—He's our very real and present hope. He's the One whose Spirit lives within us in this moment, tenderly loving, graciously guiding, and holding us reassuringly. The hope we have in Christ is unlike any other because it can never run out. He is eternal, and once we have given our hearts to Him, we are inseparable. That means no circumstance can be challenging enough, no mistake can be grave enough, no despair can be deep enough to take His love from us. This is vital to remember in our darkest hours—and we all face them in our own ways. Even when we can't sense it; even when we feel particularly doubtful, angry, frustrated, or exasperated; even those times when we just want to cry out, *Why???* (and sometimes even *do*), He is there with a very personal and steadfast love that *does not change one bit*. Let that truth be your anchor, no matter what you face. The hope you have in Him will outlast every other thing you experience in this life. In fact, it will outlast your life on this earth and carry you into that bright future where, "What God has planned for people who love Him is more than eyes have seen or ears have heard. It has never even entered our minds!" (I Corinthians 2:9 CEV).

Write about a time when God worked in your life unexpectedly, and you were reminded how much He cares about every detail of you.

What difficult things are you facing today that you've tried to sweep under the rug? Maybe it feels too insignificant or too shameful to admit or too overwhelming.

What would you say to someone you love if they were dealing with the same thing?

How can you remind yourself more often of Jesus' very real presence with you?

What do you feel is most helpful, hopeful thing you will take away from this book, and is there anyone in your life you might share it with?

Here's one question to ask yourself that can be both eye-opening and inspiring:

What am I putting my hope in these days?

What things, experiences, people do you look to for a sense of well-being in your daily life? Of course, it's not a bad thing at all for us to own things, to enjoy experiences, and invest in relationships—these are God's wonderful gifts to us! But it's important to stay aware of just how much we allow them to determine our happiness. Because we all know that nothing is guaranteed; we could wake up tomorrow without whatever it is we're depending on today. But here's the best news ever: There is not one day of your life that you will wake up without your greatest, most dependable, eternal Source of hope—God's Spirit within you. Unlike anything (or anyone) else, He is here to stay, without fail, forever. That's why cultivating your relationship with Him is the single greatest thing you can do to create a deeply joyful, peaceful, and satisfying life. Because the more you learn to look to Him for reassurance amid those little, daily things you face, the more naturally you will lean into Him when the big storms come. And we'll all face storms in this life...but never, ever alone. So, as you look back over your answers in this book, thank God for all He has revealed to you about your journey. Thank Him for the good things, experiences, and people He's blessed you with in your life. Celebrate them. Keep enjoying them. Just remind yourself often that the Giver is infinitely greater than the gifts, and all you ever need will be found in Him.

The Comfort Promises by

DaySpring

No matter what you are facing today, you can rest in knowing the Creator of the universe loves you. He loves you deeply and perfectly with absolutely no conditions. And He's made hundreds of promises to you!

Below you'll find the 100 most referenced, quoted, and memorized Bible promises. At DaySpring, we call these The Comfort Promises™—the verses we turn to again and again for encouragement, joy, and strength. For your convenience, we've provided a quick reference guide—a unique tool that makes it easy for you to find just the right comfort promises for your immediate need.

When you are **afraid . . .**

He will not allow your foot to slip;
He who keeps you will not slumber.
PSALM 121:3 NASB

Do not fear; I will help you.
ISAIAH 41:13 NIV

Draw near to God, and He will draw near to you.
JAMES 4:8 CSB

When you are **anxious . . .**

If you follow Me, you won't have to walk in darkness,
because you will have the light that leads to life.
JOHN 8:12 NLT

Don't fret or worry. Instead of worrying, pray.
PHILIPPIANS 4:6 THE MESSAGE

He never changes or casts a shifting shadow.
JAMES 1:17 NLT

When you need **assurance . . .**

He is the faithful God, keeping His covenant
of love to a thousand generations.
DEUTERONOMY 7:9 NIV

You're blessed when you're at the end of your rope.
With less of you there is more of God.
MATTHEW 5:3 THE MESSAGE

He chose us...that we would be holy
and blameless before Him.
EPHESIANS 1:4 NASB

You are saved by grace through faith...
it is God's gift.
EPHESIANS 2:8 CSB

He cares about you.
I PETER 5:7 NLT

His divine power has given us
everything required for life.
II PETER 1:3 CSB

When you need comfort . . .

The Lord is near the brokenhearted;
He saves those crushed in spirit.
PSALM 34:18 CSB

Take delight in the Lord,
and He will give you your heart's desires.
PSALM 37:4 CSB

My faithful love for you will remain.
My covenant of blessing will never be broken.
ISAIAH 54:10 NLT

I have it all planned out—plans to take care of you,
not abandon you, plans to give you the future
you hope for.
JEREMIAH 29:11 THE MESSAGE

He will rejoice over you with gladness...
He will delight in you with singing.
ZEPHANIAH 3:17 CSB

Blessed are those who mourn,
for they shall be comforted.
MATTHEW 5:4 ESV

He comforts us in all our troubles
so that we can comfort others.
II CORINTHIANS 1:4 NLT

God has chosen you and made you His holy people.
He loves you.
COLOSSIANS 3:12 ICB

When you need courage . . .

But You, Lord, are a shield around me, my glory,
and the One who lifts up my head.
PSALM 3:3 CSB

I can do all things through Christ
because He gives me strength.
PHILIPPIANS 4:13 ICB

He hears their cry for help and saves them.
PSALM 145:19 CSB

I will strengthen you, I will help you,
I will uphold you with my righteous right hand.
ISAIAH 41:10 ESV

This is what the Lord says, he who made the earth,
the Lord who formed it and established it—the Lord
is His name: "Call to me and I will answer you and tell
you great and unsearchable things you do not know."
JEREMIAH 33:2–3 NIV

The Lord is good to those who wait for Him,
to the person who seeks Him.
LAMENTATIONS 3:25 NASB

I will send you the Helper from the Father.
He is the Spirit of truth who comes from the Father.
JOHN 15:26 ICB

He hears us.
I JOHN 5:14 NASB

When you need **hope . . .**

The Lord will fight for you while you keep silent.
EXODUS 14:14 NASB

Be strong; don't give up, for your work has a reward.
II CHRONICLES 15:7 CSB

The Lord grants favor and honor;
He does not withhold the good
from those who live with integrity.
PSALM 84:11 CSB

He has planted eternity in the human heart.
ECCLESIASTES 3:11 NLT

His mercies never end.
They are new every morning.
LAMENTATIONS 3:22–23 CSB

I am the living bread....
Whoever eats this bread will live forever.
JOHN 6:51 NIV

Anyone who believes in Me will live,
even after dying.
JOHN 11:25 NLT

We have this hope as an anchor for the soul,
firm and secure.
HEBREWS 6:19 NIV

When you need **joy . . .**

Do not grieve, for the joy of the Lord is your strength.
NEHEMIAH 8:10 NIV

You will fill me with joy in Your presence.
PSALM 16:11 NIV

You turned my lament into dancing.
PSALM 30:11 CSB

Give, and it will be given to you.
LUKE 6:38 NIV

When you are **lonely . . .**

He will be with you; He will not leave you
or abandon you.
DEUTERONOMY 31:8 CSB

The Lord your God is with you wherever you go.
JOSHUA 1:9 CSB

He Himself has said,
"I will never leave you or abandon you."
HEBREWS 13:5 CSB

When you are feeling **overwhelmed . . .**

For nothing will be impossible with God.
LUKE 1:37 ESV

The God of all grace...will himself restore,
confirm, strengthen, and establish you.
I PETER 5:10 ESV

When you need **peace . . .**

The Lord gives His people strength;
the Lord blesses His people with peace.
PSALM 29:11 CSB

Peace I leave with you. My peace I give to you.
JOHN 14:27 CSB

God's peace will keep your hearts and minds
in Christ Jesus.
PHILIPPIANS 4:7 ICB

When you need **protection . . .**

You are a hiding place for me;
you preserve me from trouble.
PSALM 32:7 ESV

You protect people as a bird
protects her young under her wings.
PSALM 36:7 ICB

God has not given us a spirit of fear,
but one of power, love, and sound judgment.
II TIMOTHY 1:7 CSB

Humble yourselves before the Lord,
and He will lift you up.
JAMES 4:10 NIV

When you need **encouragement . . .**

His faithful love endures forever.
PSALM 100:5 CSB

I will be your God throughout your lifetime—
until your hair is white with age.
ISAIAH 46:4 NLT

I will give you a new heart
and put a new spirit within you.
EZEKIEL 36:26 CSB

For I am convinced that neither death nor life,
neither angels nor demons, neither the present
nor the future, nor any powers, neither height
nor depth, nor anything else in all creation,
will be able to separate us from the love of God
that is in Christ Jesus our Lord.
ROMANS 8:38–39 NIV

He will not let you be tempted beyond your ability.
I CORINTHIANS 10:13 ESV

He has created us anew in Christ Jesus,
so we can do the good things He planned for us.
EPHESIANS 2:10 NLT

When you need forgiveness . . .

I will forgive their sin and will heal their land.
II CHRONICLES 7:14 NIV

Though your sins are scarlet,
they will be as white as snow.
ISAIAH 1:18 CSB

By giving Himself completely at the Cross,
actually dying for you, Christ brought you over
to God's side and put your lives together,
whole and holy in His presence.
COLOSSIANS 1:22 THE MESSAGE

He...will forgive us our sins and purify us.
I JOHN 1:9 NIV

God, who...will bring you with great joy
into His glorious presence without a single fault.
JUDE 1:24 NLT

When you need guidance . . .

He will make your paths straight.
PROVERBS 3:6 CSB

The Lord will continually guide you.
ISAIAH 58:11 NASB

When the Spirit of truth comes,
He will guide you into all truth.
JOHN 16:13 NLT

When you need healing . . .

He heals the brokenhearted
and binds up their wounds.
PSALM 147:3 ESV

By His wounds we are healed.
ISAIAH 53:5 NIV

I will give you back your health
and heal your wounds.
JEREMIAH 30:17 NLT

When you need help . . .

I will send you rain in its season, and the ground
will yield its crops and the trees their fruit.
LEVITICUS 26:4 NIV

Day after day He bears our burdens.
PSALM 68:19 CSB

He will give His angels orders...
to protect you in all your ways.
PSALM 91:11 CSB

The Lord will guard your going out and your
coming in from this time forth and forever.
PSALM 121:8 NASB

He is a shield to those who take refuge in Him.
PROVERBS 30:5 CSB

A stronghold for the poor...
a refuge from storms
and a shade from heat.
ISAIAH 25:4 CSB

No weapon turned against you will succeed.
ISAIAH 54:17 NLT

He will strengthen you and protect you.
II THESSALONIANS 3:3 NIV

When you need **rest *and* renewal . . .**

The Lord is my shepherd, I lack nothing.
He makes me lie down in green pastures,
He leads me beside quiet waters.
PSALM 23:1–2 NIV

He renews my life; He leads me along
the right paths for His name's sake.
PSALM 23:3 CSB

He satisfies you with good things;
your youth is renewed like the eagle.
PSALM 103:5 CSB

Those who wait for the Lord will gain new strength;
they will mount up with wings like eagles,
they will run and not get tired, they will walk
and not become weary.
ISAIAH 40:31 NASB

Come to me, all who labor and are heavy laden,
and I will give you rest.
MATTHEW 11:28 ESV

The Son of Man came to find and restore the lost.
LUKE 19:10 THE MESSAGE

Jesus answered, "Everyone who drinks this water
will be thirsty again, but whoever drinks the water
I give them will never thirst. Indeed, the water
I give them will become in them a spring of water
welling up to eternal life."
JOHN 4:13–14 NIV

Our inner person is being renewed day by day.
II CORINTHIANS 4:16 CSB

If anyone is in Christ, he is a new creation.
II CORINTHIANS 5:17 CSB

When you need **strength . . .**

He gives power to the weak and strength
to the powerless.
ISAIAH 40:29 NLT

The Spirit helps us in our weakness.
ROMANS 8:26 ESV

He will keep you strong to the end so that
you will be free from all blame on the day
when our Lord Jesus Christ returns.
I CORINTHIANS 1:8 NLT

When you are **suffering . . .**

He will sustain you; He will never allow
the righteous to be shaken.
PSALM 55:22 NASB

As a father has compassion on his children,
so the Lord has compassion on those who fear Him;
for He knows how we are formed,
He remembers that we are dust.
PSALM 103:13–14 NIV

I will be with you...
When you walk through the fire,
you will not be scorched.
ISAIAH 43:2 CSB

The Lord is good, a stronghold in the day of trouble.
NAHUM 1:7 ESV

Remain in Me, and I will remain in you.
JOHN 15:4 NLT

When you need **wisdom . . .**

Continue to ask, and God will give to you.
Continue to search, and you will find.
Continue to knock, and the door will open for you.
MATTHEW 7:7 ICB

It is because of Him that you are in Christ Jesus,
who has become for us wisdom from God—
that is, our righteousness, holiness and redemption.
I CORINTHIANS 1:30 NIV

Now if any of you lacks wisdom, he should ask God...
and it will be given to him.
JAMES 1:5 CSB

When you are **worried . . .**

Your Father knows the things you need
before you ask Him.
MATTHEW 6:8 ICB

God will meet all your needs.
PHILIPPIANS 4:19 NIV

Dear Friend,

This book was prayerfully crafted with you, the reader, in mind. Every word, every sentence, every page was thoughtfully written, designed, and packaged to encourage you—right where you are this very moment. At DaySpring, our vision is to see every person experience the life-changing message of God's love. So, as we worked through rough drafts, design changes, edits, and details, we prayed for you to deeply experience His unfailing love, indescribable peace, and pure joy. It is our sincere hope that through these Truth-filled pages your heart will be blessed, knowing that God cares about you—your desires and disappointments, your challenges and dreams.

He knows. He cares. He loves you unconditionally.

BLESSINGS!
THE DAYSPRING BOOK TEAM